W9-CLL-077

10
MINUTE GUIDE TO

MICROSOFT®
EXCHANGE 4.0

by Kathy Ivens

A Division of Macmillan Computer Publishing
201 West 103rd St., Indianapolis, Indiana 46290 USA

This book is dedicated to Al McWilliams, both as a challenge to get him to read a book about computers, and as a way to acknowledge my affection for him.

Library of Congress Catalog Card Number: 96-68983

International Standard Book Number: 0-7897-0897-3

98 97   8 7 6 5 4

Interpretation of the printing code: the rightmost double-digit number is the year of the book's first printing; the rightmost single-digit number is the number of the book's printing. For example, a printing code of 96-1 shows that this copy of the book was printed during the first printing of the book in 1996.

Printed in the United States of America

Publisher Roland Elgey

Publishing Manager Lynn E. Zingraf

Editorial Services Director Elizabeth Keaffaber

Managing Editor Michael Cunningham

Acquisitions Editor Martha O'Sullivan

Technical Specialist Nadeem Muhammed

Product Development Specialist Melanie Palaisa

Production Editor Linda Seifert

Copy Editor Patricia A. Solberg

Book Designer Kim Scott

Cover Designer Dan Armstrong

Production Team Jason Carr, Christy McKay, Steph Mineart, Darlena Murray, Kelly Warner, Donna Wright

Indexer Chris Barrick

Special thanks to Michael Patten for ensuring the technical accuracy of this book.

Contents

INTRODUCTION

The 10 Minute Guide to Microsoft Exchange 4.0 is a guide for learning about the important features of this new and powerful software. Each lesson provides step-by-step instructions on a specific feature or function of Microsoft Exchange Client.

WHAT IS MICROSOFT EXCHANGE CLIENT?

Microsoft Exchange Client is the software used on network workstations in organizations that have installed Microsoft Exchange Server, a new and robust messaging software application that gives you more power than the Exchange software that came with your Windows operating system.

If you're using Microsoft Exchange Client, you're connected to a network and you use that network for sending messages. Correspondence that's conducted over a network is called e-mail, an electronic method for sending letters, memos, notes and files to other people.

The contents of this book are based on the assumption that an administrator has installed your Microsoft Exchange Client software and configured it so you can work efficiently and productively.

Some of the features you'll learn about in this book include:

- Sending and receiving e-mail, internally and outside your company
- Accessing shared information in files and folders
- Scheduling your time
- Keeping track of contacts
- Organizing To-do lists
- Delegating mail functions

- Handling messages automatically while you're out of the office

- Working at home or on the road and then synchronizing all your files

WHAT IS *The 10 Minute Guide to Microsoft Exchange 4.0?*

This *10 Minute Guide* is a quick way to learn about the important features of Microsoft Exchange Client. Concise lessons guide you through specific tasks, giving you hands-on practice. Each lesson should take about 10 minutes to complete.

You can start at the beginning and go through all the lessons, or jump directly to a lesson that interests you.

The book assumes you have some experience with Windows, that you know how to use a mouse, and understand the way to use menus and toolbars.

For additional help, there are three special elements throughout this book, each identified with its own icon:

Timesaver Tips are suggestions for faster completion of a task and some useful information about the task.

Plain English elements define Microsoft Exchange Client terminology, or computer jargon.

Panic Button icons give some insight into avoiding potential problems.

Conventions Used in This Book

This book also uses the following conventions to help you distinguish important information:

What you type   Things that you have to type appear in bold, italic type.

Things you select   Keys that you need to press and items that you need to select appear in colored type.

On-screen text   On-screen messages from Microsoft Exchange appear in bold type.

Acknowledgments

I owe an enormous thank you to Martha O'Sullivan and Melanie Palaisa, both of Que, for being incredibly professional, helpful, and supportive throughout the rush to get this book into your hands. Linda Seifert's expert editing and administrative skills guaranteed me that I won't be embarrassed that you're reading this book. Michael Patten was efficient and effective with technical editing and he has my deep appreciation.

Lou Iannamorelli's expert input into the philosophy and content of this book was extremely helpful and I offer my gratitude to him.

Trademarks

All terms mentioned in this book that are known to be trademarks have been appropriately capitalized. Que cannot attest to the accuracy of this information. Use of a term in this book should not be regarded as affecting the validity of any trademark or service mark.

WE'D LIKE TO HEAR FROM YOU!

As part of our continuing effort to produce books of the highest possible quality, Que would like to hear your comments. To stay competitive, we *really* want you, as a computer book reader and user, to let us know what you like or dislike most about this book or other Que products.

You can mail comments, ideas, or suggestions for improving future editions to the address below, or send us a fax at (317) 581-4663. For the online inclined, Macmillan Computer Publishing has a forum on CompuServe (type **GO QUEBOOKS** at any prompt) through which our staff and authors are available for questions and comments. The address of our Internet site is **http://www.mcp.com**.

In addition to exploring our forum, please feel free to contact me personally to discuss your opinions of this book: on CompuServe, I'm at **73353,2061**, and on the Internet, I'm **mpalaisa@ que.mcp.com**.

Thanks in advance—your comments will help us to continue publishing the best books available on computer topics in today's market.

Melanie Palaisa
Product Development Specialist
Que Corporation
201 W. 103rd Street
Indianapolis, Indiana 46290
USA

WELCOME TO EXCHANGE

In this lesson, you'll learn how Microsoft Exchange Server handles the interaction between your computer (workstation) and the server that runs the main part of the software.

UNDERSTANDING MICROSOFT EXCHANGE SERVER

Your Microsoft Exchange software is part of Microsoft Exchange Server, a network-wide system that's been installed in your company to handle messaging, scheduling, and other exchanges of information among employees, as well as between employees and the outside world.

Microsoft Exchange Server consists of two components:

- *Server.* This component runs on a Microsoft Exchange server computer. A server that provides core services for Microsoft Exchange Server must run on the Windows NT operating system, but it can communicate with servers that use other operating systems.

- *Client.* This component runs on each user's workstation.

There are a number of elements within each of these two components, and they all work together to accomplish tasks across a network or a group of networks.

Servers   Servers are computers that have some form of authority over other, connected computers. For example, servers hold the names and passwords of all the users who have workstations linked to the server, and sometimes they hold software that is accessed by all the connected users.

Clients   Clients are the computers used by the people who do the work. (Client computers are connected to servers, usually by cable, and are called workstations.)

THE EXCHANGE CLIENT SOFTWARE

The client software for Microsoft Exchange Server runs on the following operating systems:

- Windows 3.1

- Windows for Workgroups 3.11

- Windows NT 3.51 Workstation

- Windows NT 4.0 Workstation

- Windows 95

While the client software also runs on DOS (version 5.0 or later), only messaging functions are supported and all other features are inaccessible.

The Windows NT Workstation and Windows 95 versions of Exchange Server Client are the most commonly used. They also look and behave the same, so throughout this book I'll discuss Exchange Server Client from that perspective. If you're using Windows 3.x, your Exchange software may look slightly different, but the functions will operate the same.

HOW CLIENT AND SERVER SOFTWARE WORK TOGETHER

Microsoft Exchange Server is a *modular* client/server system. It is modular because a number of different components are available, so each company can install and use the features it needs. It is client/server-based because the performance of tasks takes place at both the client and the server.

If there is a request for information to perform a client process, such as getting a name from the company's e-mail address book, the information is sent to the client. The client can then use the data to complete a process, such as composing a message. Figure 1.1 illustrates the procedures when a client requests this type of information from the server.

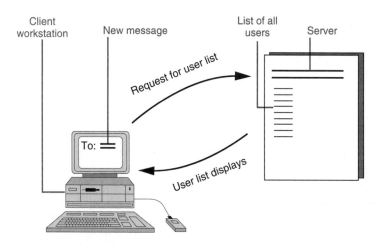

FIGURE 1.1 Clicking the button that displays the list of names sends a request to the server that holds that list. When the server sends the list to the user's workstation, the user selects one or more names and continues the task without any further input from the server.

When a client sends a request to a server, if the completion of the task requires a server-based process, the server will proceed with the task. For example, the client might ask the server to deliver a message to another user. Figure 1.2 shows that server process.

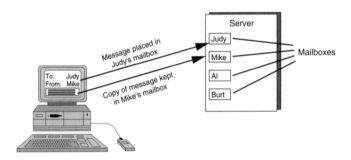

FIGURE 1.2   After preparing a message at the workstation, the user sends it to the recipient. This causes the message to be sent to the server, where all the mailboxes are stored, and the message is placed in the recipient's mailbox (a copy is stored in the sender's mailbox).

UNDERSTANDING OBJECTS

Object is the term used by Exchange to describe the way the elements in your Exchange software are viewed. Every element is treated as an object, including files, folders, messages, lists, and even computers. Objects are represented on your screen as icons.

Even though you see many objects in the Exchange window when you're using the software, they aren't all stored in the same place—they just display themselves to you in one place. You can't tell by looking at an object where it is stored.

Your mailbox is located on a server that is running Microsoft Exchange. You are connected to that server (usually by cable). The server receives the messages you've composed and they are sent to the server-based mailboxes of the recipients. When other users send mail to you, it is placed in your mailbox.

If your company has multiple locations, and therefore has installed multiple Microsoft Exchange servers, the administrators have devised a system of delivering mail among all the servers.

Your mailbox name appears on the list of users all through your company, and the mailbox names displayed on your computer include everyone in your company. When you send a message, you can't tell where the recipient is, or to which server that recipient is attached, but it doesn't matter. Microsoft Exchange Server follows a route from server to server to get and deliver your mail.

Figure 1.3 shows how all the users end up being displayed on your computer's monitor as one group, regardless of their location or to which server they're connected.

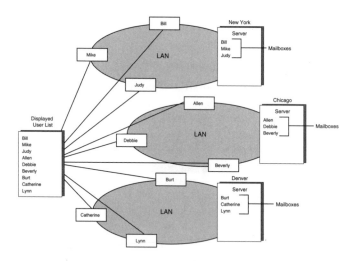

FIGURE 1.3 All the networks a company maintains have servers that are linked (usually by telephone lines) so each user sees every mailbox available in the company, no matter where the individual mailboxes are stored.

In this lesson you learned how the Microsoft Exchange Server and the Exchange Client software work together, and what it means to be working in a client/server environment. In the next lesson, you learn how to open and close the Microsoft Exchange Client software, and you'll also learn how to use your mailbox.

2

STARTING AND QUITTING EXCHANGE

In this lesson, you'll learn how to start and end a session in Exchange, and how to navigate through your mailbox folders.

STARTING EXCHANGE

To launch the Exchange client software, use one of the following methods:

- If you are using Windows 95 or Windows NT 4.0, double-click the Inbox icon on your desktop (see Figure 2.1).

FIGURE 2.1 In Windows 95 or Windows NT 4.0, the Inbox icon launches the client software for Exchange.

- If you are using Windows NT 3.51 or Windows 3.x, open the Exchange program group and double-click the Exchange program icon (see Figure 2.2).

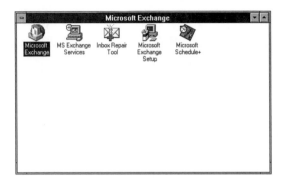

FIGURE 2.2 In Windows NT 3.51 or Windows 3.x, the Exchange icon is inside the Exchange program group.

THE VIEWER

The window that opens when you start Exchange is called the Viewer. It contains the elements found in Windows software applications, such as a title bar, a menu bar, a toolbar, and a status bar. However, there are some additional elements that make the Viewer a bit different when compared to other software windows (see Figure 2.3).

The Viewer is an object-based window, and displays objects in a hierarchical view. The viewer is divided into two panes. The pane on the left displays the folders you have access to and the pane on the right shows the contents of the folder that's been selected in the left pane. The right pane also contains column headings to indicate the information available for the displayed contents. The column headings change according to the type of objects being displayed.

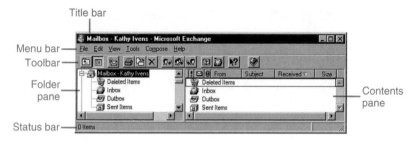

FIGURE 2.3   The Exchange viewer is a bit different from most software windows—it's divided into panes and contains objects.

THE MAILBOX

The Mailbox object that displays in the left pane represents your server-based mailbox into which messages are placed. Your mailbox has four folders (you can add more folders, which is shown in Lesson 13).

THE INBOX FOLDER

The Inbox folder receives the mail that's sent to you. When you highlight the Inbox in the folder pane, the contents pane displays all the messages in your Inbox (see Figure 2.4). Incidentally, the number in parentheses next to the Inbox indicates the number of unopened (unread) messages. It does not necessarily represent the total number of messages in your Inbox because you may not have disposed of previously opened messages. Notice that the status bar indicates the number of unread messages and the total number of messages in the Inbox.

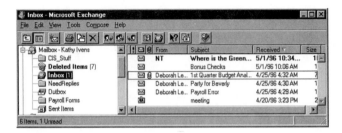

FIGURE 2.4   Click the Inbox object to see the messages waiting for you.

THE COLUMNS IN THE CONTENTS PANE

There are a number of columns in the contents pane to indicate information about the displayed objects. By default, the columns for received messages are (from left to right):

- **Importance**   This is the priority the sender places on this message (high, low, or normal).

- **Item Type**   This is the type of message. Message types are discussed later in this lesson.

- **Attachment**   Files or other objects can be attached to a message

- **From**   This is the name of the sender.

- **Subject**   This is the subject of the message, which is decided on by the sender.

- **Received**   This is the date and time the message was placed in your mailbox.

- **Size**   This is the size, in kilobytes, of the message.

Configure the Columns   You can add or remove column headings and change the order in which columns display by choosing View, Columns and following the instructions for changing the column display.

Re-sort the Message List   If you click a column title, the messages are sorted according to the selected column title. By default, the messages are displayed in a sorting scheme based on the received date (the list is in descending order starting with the most recent date and time). There is a small arrow displayed on the column header that is currently being used for sorting the list.

THE LIST OF MESSAGES

The display of received messages in the contents pane is designed to give you some information about each message:

- A plain envelope in the Item Type column represents a standard message, or you may see icons representing faxes, or special forms that have been designed for use in your company.

- An envelope with a padlock on it represents an encrypted message (called a "sealed" message) that requires a password to open.

- An envelope with a pen on it represents a message containing a digital signature (called a "signed" message) and requires a password to open.

- A paper clip in the Attachment column means there is an attachment to the message.

- A red exclamation point in the Importance column indicates the sender has marked the message for high priority.

- A down arrow in the Importance column indicates the sender has marked the message for low priority.

- Messages that are bolded are new and have not been opened.

Understanding Signed and Sealed Messages

Signed and sealed are Microsoft Exchange terms for special security measures that can be applied to messages:

- A signed message is one in which the sender has added an attribute that requires a recipient password. This ensures that only the recipient can open the message.

- A sealed message is one in which the contents are encrypted. A password is required to open it and read it.

These functions are part of the Advanced Security features of Microsoft Exchange Server and are not automatically available. If Advanced Security has been enabled on your Microsoft Exchange system, your system administrator will give you the information you need to apply security measures to your messages.

The Deleted Items Folder

Deleting a message in Exchange is a bit different than deleting files from other Windows facilities, such as File Manager or Explorer. When you highlight a file and press Del (or choose Delete from the File menu), there is no confirmation message displayed, such as **Are You Sure?** or **Do You Really Want To Delete This File?** The message just disappears from the list in the contents pane. It's not really deleted however, it's merely moved to the Deleted Items folder.

You can rescue your deleted messages before they disappear permanently. Information about handling deleted messages is found in Lesson 11.

THE OUTBOX FOLDER

The Outbox is the container that holds messages you've sent until those messages are delivered to the server. The system checks the Outbox for mail to send messages, either immediately or at a specified time, depending on the choices you make. You can delete a message from the Outbox if you change your mind about sending it.

THE SENT ITEMS FOLDER

After you send a message, a copy is placed in the container called the Sent Items Folder. This is useful if you need to be reminded about the original message when you receive a reply from the recipient.

There are instances when you receive a message in response to your own e-mail, and the text of the message you receive consists of a single word like "Yes" or "Thursday." The trick is to remember the question you asked that engendered that answer. Looking in the Sent Items folder saves you the embarrassment of having to ask your correspondent what the original question was to make sense of the answer.

QUITTING EXCHANGE

There are two methods you can use to quit Exchange. Regardless of which option you use, your Microsoft Exchange Client software closes and you don't have access to its features. However, the method you use to quit has an effect on any other messaging applications that may be running on your computer.

Messaging Application Software that uses the messaging features provided by the operating system is called Messaging Application Programming Interface (MAPI). MAPI provides addressing, sending, receiving, and storing functions for messages. Software programmers use these functions to add messaging features to software. For example, there are word processors that provide some levels of messaging, enabling you to send documents to other network users while you are using the word processor (without opening Microsoft Exchange Client).

* Choose File, Exit to quit Exchange software. This closes the Microsoft Exchange Client but leaves any other messaging applications running.

* Choose File, Exit and Log Off to close Microsoft Exchange Client and all other messaging applications.

In this lesson you learned about opening and closing Exchange, and gained some understanding about Exchange's appearance. You also learned about the components of your mailbox. In the next lesson you will learn how to use the Help files in Exchange.

GETTING HELP

*In this lesson you'll learn how to use the
Help feature in Exchange to get assistance
as you perform tasks. You'll
also learn how you can add your own notes to
the information you find in the Help files.*

FINDING HELP

This lesson discusses the Microsoft Exchange Server help features
found in the Help Topics dialog box. To access this dialog box,
choose Help, Microsoft Exchange Help Topics. The Help Topics
dialog box is displayed, as shown in Figure 3.1. The Help Topics
dialog box has three tabs available so you can choose the way you
search for help. The help features available on each of these tabs
are discussed here.

FIGURE 3.1 The Help Topics dialog box.

No matter which tab you use, you end up with the same contents. Which tab you choose depends on how you want to search for help:

- Use the Contents tab to get an overview of a topic. This is useful if you want to understand how a feature works.

- Use the Index tab to find information about a broad topic by name, such as Outbox, Print, and so on.

- Use the Find tab to see all the topics that contain a specific word. When you enter the word, a listing of the index topics that contain that word is displayed.

THE CONTENTS TAB

The Contents tab lists all the Help topics, arranged by topic. A book icon is located to the left of each topic. To open a book follow these steps:

1. Click the book icon next to the category you want to open, then choose Open. When the book opens, its chapters (the page icons with the question marks) are listed (see Figure 3.2). When the book is open, the Open button changes to a Close button, which you can click on to close the book.

2. To get to the contents, use one of these choices:

   - To display the Help page of the category you want, click   the page icon , then choose Display. The Help page displays a detailed explanation of the topic (you'll learn   more about the contents of the Help page later in this lesson).

   - To print a chapter, select it and choose Print.

   - To print a book, select it and choose Print. A book can contain many chapters, so it might be faster and less wasteful to print only the specific chapters you really need.

FIGURE 3.2   The chapters for each book display so you can pick the one you need.

3. Click the Contents button to return to the Contents tab.

4. Click the Close button (the **X** in the upper-right corner of the dialog box) to close the Help facility.

THE INDEX TAB

When you click the Index tab in the Help Topics dialog box, the Help window changes to display the Index, which looks like a book index (see Figure 3.3). Entries are listed alphabetically, with subtopics indented below the major topics. All the major topics for which there are pages in the Help books are included.

To find a help topic using the Index tab, follow these steps:

1. In the **Type the first few letters of the word you're looking for** text box, type the first letters or words of the Help topic you're looking for.

2. As you type, the index list jumps to the first listing that matches the characters you're typing and highlights that topic, as shown in Figure 3.4.

FIGURE 3.3   The Help Index tab.

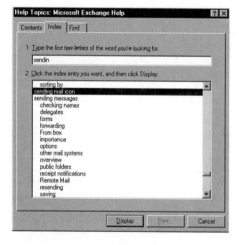

FIGURE 3.4   As you type, the index listings move to the topics that match the letters you're typing.

3. (Optional) Rather than type the topic in the text box, you can scroll through the index listings, either to get an idea of the available topics, or to find a specific topic.

4. When you get to the index section you want, select the topic and choose Display to see the information or Print to print it.

THE FIND TAB

The Find tab is useful for locating Help entries when you're not sure of their Index titles. You can type a word and see all the topics that contain that word in their contents.

The first time you use the Find tab, you must create a database of words and Help files that Find uses to locate the help topics you want. Don't worry, Exchange provides a Find Setup Wizard to help you through the process.

To create the Find database and use the Find feature, follow these steps:

1. Click the Find tab in the Help topics dialog box. The Find Setup Wizard appears as shown in Figure 3.5.

FIGURE 3.5 The Find Setup Wizard.

2. Choose the database configuration (described next) by clicking the option button next to the configuration you want. Click Next.

3. After making your selection, follow the Wizard's easy
instructions to complete the creation of the database for
the Find tab.

THE DATABASE CHOICES

There are three choices available for configuring the database:

 Choosing a Database Option   Don't worry about making the wrong choice. You can re-establish this database
with different choices by clicking the Rebuild button on
the Find tab. The Find Setup Wizard walks you through
the process.

Minimize database size.   Use this option to
create only a database, with no additional features
except for the ability to search for words.

Maximize search capabilities.   Use this option
to create a database that has added features that
enable you to search for a topic, then move to other
similar topics without entering a new word to search
on. This database is much larger and takes longer to
load when you want to use the Find tab, so don't
choose this option unless you have found that working with the Minimize database size choice isn't
providing the services you need.

Customize search capabilities.   Use this option
to make advanced decisions about how to establish
the database, such as which Help files to use, whether
to include topics that are not part of an Index section
(some definitions are not indexed), the ability to
search for phrases instead of words, and the ability
to mark a section and then search for similar sections
even if those similar sections don't contain the word
you typed. This database is large and is much slower

to use, so if you don't need these capabilities don't select this choice.

After the Find database has been created, you can use the Find feature by following these steps:

1. In the Help Topics dialog box, click the Find tab to display it, as shown in Figure 3.6.

2. In section 1, **Type the word(s) you want to find**, type the words or phrase in which you are interested.

3. As you type, matching characters are displayed in the **Select some matching words to narrow your search** box. Choose one or more words that most closely match the topic for which you are looking.

4. Next go to the **Click a topic, then click Display** box. The Help page for that topic is displayed (see Figure 3.7). You'll learn more about the contents of the Help page next.

5. (Optional) If you want to, you can choose Print to have a permanent reference.

Change the Way Find Works To modify the behavior of the Find tab, choose Options. The Find Options dialog box appears and you can change the way the Find feature functions—the choices are self-explanatory.

UNDERSTANDING THE CONTENTS OF A HELP PAGE

After you've used one of the methods described earlier in this lesson to choose the specific Help topic you want to examine, a Help Topic page displays. Most Help pages have more than helpful text—there are additional features and functions so you can get even more help (see Figure 3.7).

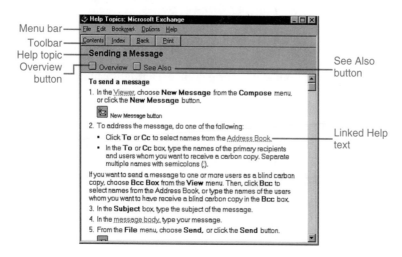

FIGURE 3.7 A typical Help page.

The following sections describe the Help page shown in
Figure 3.7.

Help Page Menu Bar

You can use the options on the menu bar to perform tasks or
access features. All the choices on all the menu items are not
described here (although you may want to explore that when you
have some time). Here are some of the most useful commands:

> **Annotate.** You can use the Annotate command to
> add your own notes or comments to the displayed
> Help topic. Choose Edit, Annotate. The Annotate
> dialog box appears. In the text box under **Current
> annotation**, type your notes, then click Save to close
> the dialog box and return to the Help page.
>
> After you've added an annotation to a Help page, a
> paper clip icon appears to the left of the first sentence
> of the contents. The next time you display this Help
> page, you can click on the paper clip to see your note.
>
> **Bookmarks.** Bookmarks are used to mark those
> pages you think you might want to return to fre-
> quently. The first time you open the Bookmark menu,
> it contains only one choice, Define. Just click OK to
> create the bookmark.

After you've created a bookmark for a page, it's added to
the Bookmark menu. To find a favorite Help page, choose
Bookmark and click on the bookmark of the page you need.
You'll move to that Help page immediately.

THE HELP TOPIC TOOLBAR

The toolbar buttons on the Help Topic page perform the following functions:

- Contents returns you to the Contents tab of the Help system.

- Index returns you to the Index tab of the Help system.

- Back moves you back to the previous Help Topic page (it's greyed out and inaccessible if you are on the first page that displayed after you selected a topic).

- Print prints the currently displayed topic.

For some reason, there is no toolbar button to return to the Find tab of the Help system—I find the easiest way to get there from here is to click on Index, then click on the Find tab.

OVERVIEW

Some topic pages have an Overview choice below the topic title. Choosing this displays an overview of the general topic that the current page is a part of.

SEE ALSO

Click on See Also to see other topics that include a reference to, or additional information about, the current topic.

LINKED HELP TEXT

You can click on any text that is underlined (it's also in a different color) and see its definition. Text underlined with dashes is linked to definitions, and text underlined with a solid line is linked to other topics.

FINDING HELP IN EXCHANGE'S DIALOG BOXES

This lesson has discussed the main Help system, but it's important to note that as you use the features in Microsoft Exchange Client, most of the dialog boxes and windows you use also have a Help feature.

If a dialog box has a Help button, click on it to see specific help about the options on that dialog box.

If any dialog box has a question mark in the upper-right corner, it means that the "What's This?" feature is active. To learn about any part of the dialog box, click on the question mark, then click on any title or text in the dialog box to see its definition. The presence of the question mark also means you can right-click on any title or text to bring up a small box that says **What's This?**, then click on the small box to see the definition.

In this lesson you learned how to find specific Help topics, and how to take advantage of special features available on the Help pages in Exchange. In the next lesson, you'll learn about the Global Address List.

USING THE GLOBAL ADDRESS LIST

*In this lesson, you'll learn how to find
a user through the Global Address list. E-mail addresses and what they
mean are also discussed.*

THE PURPOSE OF THE GLOBAL ADDRESS LIST

Before you learn how to create mail messages, it's important that
you know about the Global Address List and how to access and
use it. The Global Address List is a directory of all users to whom
you can address mail. The list is maintained by the administrators
of your Exchange system and is stored on the Microsoft Exchange
server. Besides listing individuals, there may be folders included
in the Global Address List, and you can send messages or files to
those folders.

DISPLAYING THE GLOBAL ADDRESS LIST

The Global Address List can be displayed from two places in your
Microsoft Exchange Client software and the two resulting displays
are slightly different in appearance. There also are some differ-
ences in the way you can use each one.

DISPLAYING THE LIST FROM THE TOOLS MENU

Choose Tools, Address Book to display the Address Book dialog
box (see Figure 4.1).

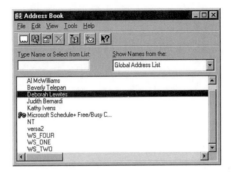

FIGURE 4.1 The Address Book dialog box displays the Global Address List.

You cannot add or delete any names from the Global Address List because it is administered by Microsoft Exchange Server administrators, but you can use the menu options and toolbar to get information about any user on the list.

You can get additional information about anyone in the listing by selecting the user and clicking on the Properties button on the toolbar (or you can double-click on the listing). The Properties dialog box displays any additional information that is available for this user (see Figure 4.2).

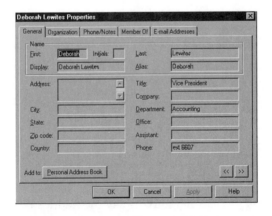

FIGURE 4.2 If the administrators have added any optional information to the user information, you can view it.

From the Properties dialog box, you can obtain any of the following information about any person on the Global Address List:

- Any distribution lists that this member is on can be found by selecting the Member Of tab (distribution lists are discussed in Lesson 6).

- You can check the exact e-mail address for the user by selecting the E-mail Address tab. This is useful if the user is a custom recipient (someone outside your company). More information about e-mail addresses is found later in this lesson.

- You can copy any name on the Global Address List to your own personal address list, which is discussed in the next lesson.

Custom Recipient   A user listed in an address book who is reached through another system, not an employee of your company. Someone reached through the Internet, CompuServe, or a main frame message system such as PROFS, is a custom recipient.

DISPLAYING THE LIST FROM A MESSAGE FORM

When you compose a message (by clicking the New Message button), you can display the Global Address List by clicking on the TO: button in the New Message form (see Figure 4.3). You can select one or more users as recipients of your message. Lesson 7 explains how to select a recipient when you create a new message.

UNDERSTANDING E-MAIL ADDRESSES

When you send mail, you're sending it to an address that is unique to the recipient, and to receive mail, your e-mail address has to be known to the sender. There are many e-mail address types and Microsoft Exchange Server provides features to ensure that your administrators have a way to establish whatever address type the users in your company may need.

The e-mail address configured for you is accessible to other users in your company. Like you, they see a list of users when they compose a message, and choose your name from the list when they want to send you a message.

However, the list that's displayed when users are working in Microsoft Exchange Client is not really a list of e-mail addresses; it's a list of shortcut references called *display names*.

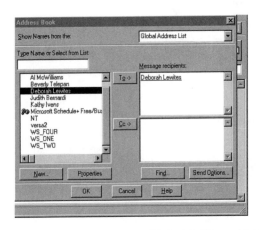

FIGURE 4.3   Select a user from the Global Address List, then choose To: to add the user as a recipient for a new message.

USING THE FIND TOOL

Most companies have a long list of e-mail addresses and you can click on the Find button to speed up the search for a particular user. When the Find dialog box displays, you can provide information to help the Find tool locate the user you need (see Figure 4.4). To find a user, the more information you fill out, the narrower and faster the search. Generally, unless a user needs to send mail to someone outside their company, they do not need to know the complete address to send them mail. They only need to know the alias or display name.

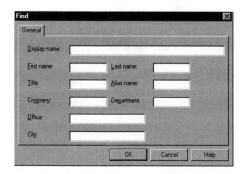

FIGURE 4.4   Each information box that's filled out by you helps to narrow the search, and is therefore more efficient.

In this lesson,, you learned about the Global Address List that is used to send messages to users inside your company and outside your company. In the next lesson, you'll learn how to create your own personal address list.

USING PERSONAL ADDRESS BOOKS

In this lesson, you'll learn how to create a personal address book, so you can keep your own list of message recipients.

CREATING A PERSONAL ADDRESS BOOK

A personal address book (PAB) is a list of addresses which you can create, customize, and use for sending messages. This is your own personal list and is not visible to any other users. You can add and delete names as necessary to keep your PAB up to date and useful.

Before you can begin adding names to your PAB, you have to create it. This is a two step process:

- Add Personal Address Book to the list of Microsoft Exchange Client services you want to use.
- Create the Personal Address Book.

ADDING THE PAB TO EXCHANGE CLIENT SERVICES

By default, the installation process for Microsoft Exchange Client does not give you the option to have PABs. The administrators who installed your software might have added this option for you, but if they didn't you can add it yourself easily.

To see if you have a PAB option, or to add the option, choose Tools, Services, to display the Services dialog box (see Figure 5.1).

FIGURE 5.1   The Services dialog box.

If Personal Address Book is listed, you're all set. If not, follow
these steps to add the PAB to your Microsoft Exchange Client
software and customize some of its features:

1. Choose Add from the Services dialog box to display the
   Add Service to Profile dialog box (see Figure 5.2).

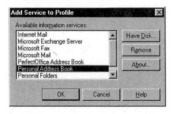

FIGURE 5.2   The Add Service dialog box.

2. Select Personal Address Book.

3. Choose OK. The Personal Address Book Properties dialog
   box is displayed.

> **TIP** If the PAB service was already listed in your Services dialog box, you can see the PAB Properties dialog box by selecting Personal Address Book from the Services list and choosing Properties.

4. (Optional) There are some configuration items you can change in the PAB Properties dialog box to customize your PAB to your own tastes and habits:

- You can use the Path box to change the name of the PAB file from Mailbox to any other name (perhaps your own name), but make sure you keep the file extension .PAB.

- You can change the way names are listed (and alphabetized) by choosing First name or Last name.

- You can use the Notes tab to write yourself a note or make a comment about this PAB (usually not a necessary item, unless you're planning to create multiple PABs).

5. After you have finished making changes, or if you're perfectly happy with the default configuration, choose OK to close the PAB Properties dialog box.

If this is the session in which you added the PAB service, Exchange will display a message telling you that your PAB will not be available for use until you exit and log off your current Exchange session. This is because the services available for you when you start Exchange are determined by the software as it first starts up (it reads the list in the Services dialog box). When you started this Exchange session, the PAB was not listed in the Services, so you can't use it. Next time you start the software, it will be listed. If you want to use the PAB right away, exit, log off, and start Exchange again.

ADDING LISTINGS TO YOUR PAB

To add listings to your PAB, copy them from the Global Address List. To do this, follow these steps:

1. Choose Tools, Address Book to display the Address Book dialog box.

2. Be sure the selection **Global Address List** is showing in the Show names from text box. If it's not, click the down arrow on the right and select it from the drop-down list.

3. Select a name from the list.

4. Click on the Add to Personal Address Book button on the toolbar (see Figure 5.3).

5. To look at the PAB listings, click on the arrow to the right of the **Show Names from the** box on the Address Book dialog box, and select Personal Address Book. The listings in your PAB are displayed.

FIGURE 5.3   Select a name in the Global Address List and copy it to your Personal Address Book.

6. When you've added all the names you want to your PAB, click the Close button to exit the Address Book dialog box.

That's all there is to it.

Note that if you opted to keep your PAB by Last Name, as the listings (which are sorted by first name by default) are moved into your PAB, they are re-sorted and displayed by Last Name.

TIP   **Copying Multiple Listings**   You can copy several names at a time to your Personal Address Book by selecting the first name, then holding down the Ctrl key as you select additional names. When you click the Add to Personal Address Book button, all the highlighted entries are copied. If you want to copy a group of contiguous names, select the first one, then move your mouse pointer to the last one you want to use, and hold down the Shift key as you click on the final name.

USING THE PERSONAL ADDRESS BOOK

Because your PAB contains listings for the recipients you most frequently send mail to, it's going to be faster to use it to find the recipient you need, rather than scroll through all the names in the Global Address List.

You can now call up an address book in one of two ways:

- Choose Tools, Address Book.

or

- Open the New Message window, click the down arrow next to the **Show Names From** box, and choose Personal Address Book.

In this lesson you learned how to create a personal address book, and how to add names to it. In the next lesson, you'll learn how to create distribution lists so you can send messages to groups instead of one person at a time.

USING DISTRIBUTION LISTS

*In this lesson, you'll learn how to use
distribution lists to send messages to a group of recipients.*

CREATING PERSONAL DISTRIBUTION LISTS

A distribution list is a collection of recipients who are grouped
together for some logical reason. The distribution list displays as a
single entity in an address book, and is addressed as a single recipient. When that recipient receives a message, the distribution
is automatically expanded to include every recipient on the list.
There may be multiple distribution lists in the Global Address
List.

If you often send messages to the same group of people, you
should create a personal distribution list (PDL). A PDL is displayed
as a recipient in your personal address book. Some common uses
for distribution lists are:

- You have a group of employees that reports to you and
  frequently have to send messages to them

- You are part of a team for a project and all team members
  frequently exchange messages

- You have regular reports due to certain management
  people

The administrators of your Microsoft Exchange Server system may
also create global distribution lists for everyone to use. These lists
appear in the Global Address List.

To create a personal distribution list, follow these steps:

1. Choose Tools, Address Book (or click on the Address Book button on the toolbar) to display the Address Book dialog box.

2. Choose File from the Address Book dialog box menu bar, then choose New Entry (or click on the New Entry button on the toolbar).

3. From the New Entry dialog box list of entry types, choose Personal Distribution List, then choose OK. The New Personal Distribution List Properties dialog box appears, as shown in Figure 6.1.

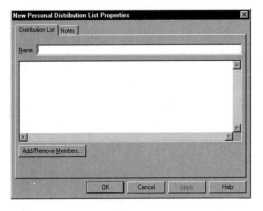

FIGURE 6.1 The New Personal Distribution List Properties dialog box.

4. In the New Personal Distribution List Properties dialog box, type a name for the distribution list in the **Name** text box. It's helpful to give your list a name that reminds you of the membership, such as "Project X team."

Friendly Reminder Click the Notes tab to add reminders and comments to yourself about this list's origin and
use.

5. Click Add/Remove Members to add recipients to the distribution list.

6. When you choose Add/Remove Members, the Edit New
   Personal Distribution List Members dialog box appears
   (see Figure 6.2).

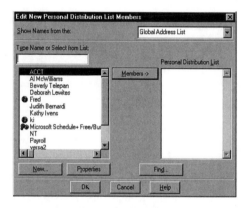

FIGURE 6.2   The Edit New Personal Distribution List Members
dialog box.

7. (Optional) By default, the Global Address List is displayed,
   but you can change that to your personal address book
   by clicking the arrow to the right of the **Show Names
   from the** box at the top of the dialog box.

8. Double-click on names to add recipients from the address
   list to your personal distribution list. The names are
   transferred to the right pane. Choose OK when you are
   finished.

When you've finished creating your personal distribution list, it appears as a recipient in your personal address book (see Figure 6.3). The listing is different, because its display is in bold type and there is an icon to the left of the entry (the icon is a picture of two people).

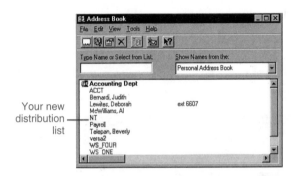

Your new distribution list

FIGURE 6.3   Distribution lists are displayed with the other entries in your personal address book.

ADD LISTS TO LISTS

You can create as many personal distribution lists as you need, and you can even add existing distribution lists to new lists. If, for example, you have a personal distribution list for all the members of a project team, and you are creating a list of people to whom you send periodic summary reports about the project, add the project team distribution list to the new list. That way you don't have to enter each recipient on the project team. In computer jargon, including a list in a list is called *nesting* or *nested lists* and Microsoft Exchange Server supports nested lists.

USING GLOBAL AND PERSONAL DISTRIBUTION LISTS

After they're created and appear in an address book, distribution lists are handled exactly the same as individual recipients. When you indicate the recipient for a message, you can just indicate the distribution list. You don't have to worry about the individual members of the distribution list receiving the message; Microsoft Exchange Server will take care of it for you.

If you're not sure of the membership of a list (especially one in the Global Address List, because you didn't create it), you can click on the distribution list and choose Properties from any dialog box or window in which the list is displayed (which could be while you are creating a new message, examining an address book, or seeing a list in any other way).

If you are looking at the Properties of a personal distribution list; you can add or delete members at any time, even while you are creating a message. You cannot change the distribution lists that display in the Global Address List because they are controlled by the system administrators.

In this lesson you learned how to create and use distribution lists for quicker messaging. In the next lesson you'll learn how to create and send a message.

COMPOSING AND SENDING MESSAGES

In this lesson, you'll learn how to compose a message, identify all recipients of the message, and send the message.

COMPOSING A MESSAGE

Composing an e-mail message is similar to writing a letter and sending it to someone via the United States Postal Service. You create text, you address it with an accurate address, and sometimes you even write a note on the envelope to indicate something special about the contents inside, such as "personal" or "urgent."

The biggest difference between e-mail and USPS mail is the speed at which your message is delivered to the recipient. After you've used e-mail and gotten used to its almost instantaneous delivery system, you'll begin to understand why computer users have adopted the jargon "snail mail" for the USPS.

When you begin the process of composing a message in Microsoft Exchange Client, you're facing three steps, all of which are quite easy:

- Fill out the message header
- Write the message
- Send the message

Message Header The message header is the top part of the message form, where you insert the name(s) of the recipient, the subject, and other information about the message. The header information displays in the Inbox when a message is received.

CREATING THE MESSAGE HEADER

The message header typically includes all the recipients of the message and the subject of the message.

There are three ways a recipient can receive a message:

- They can be the primary recipient, in which case their name(s) are listed in the **To** text box of the message.

- They can receive a carbon copy, or Cc, of the message, in which case, their name(s) are listed in the **Cc** text box of the message. Names listed in the **Cc** text box appear in the message header of each recipient.

- The recipient can receive a blind carbon copy (Bcc) of the message. In this case, the names of people receiving a BCC do not appear in the message headers of the other recipients, and the primary recipient(s) do not know who received the blind carbon copy.

When you type the name of the recipient, make sure it is spelled exactly how it appears in the address list.

The subject of your message is also very important because recipients can use it to search through messages looking for specific information. In fact, if you save the messages you send, you might also have a need to search for particular subjects. There also may be occasions when either you or the recipients need to gather similar messages and sort them so that messages with similar subjects are listed together. Therefore, try to make your wording as relevant and specific as you can. For example, entering

Project X Budget is better than ***Notes about the budget for
the project***.

To create a header for a new message, follow these steps:

1. Click the New Message button on the toolbar (or choose
   Compose, New Message), which brings up the New Message
   dialog box, shown in Figure 7.1.

FIGURE 7.1   The New Message dialog box.

2. Enter the names of the primary recipients in the **To** text
   box (the insertion point is positioned in the To text box
   by default). There are two ways to enter recipient names:

   • Type the name(s) into the **To** box, separating
     multiplerecipients with a semicolon (;).

   • Click on the To button to display the Address Book
     dialog box (see Figure 7.2). Choose an address list,
     then select the recipient(s).

3. Click on a name, then click the To button (or the Cc button) to place the recipient into the appropriate section.
   When you have finished inserting recipients, click OK.

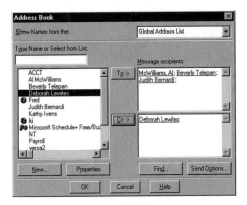

FIGURE 7.2   The Address Book dialog box.

TIP

Check Your Entries   If you opt to type the names into the recipient boxes, you must be careful to enter each name exactly as it appears in the address list. To be sure you haven't made a mistake, after you've entered the names you can choose Check Names from the Tools menu. Exchange matches each typed entry against the list of known mailboxes and notifies you when there's an entry that has no match (and offers a suggested alternative). Once the entry is confirmed, it is underlined.

Last Name First?   Don't worry about entering the last name first (or vice versa), even if your address list is established differently. Exchange figures it out. The **To** box displays the recipient the way your address book has it.

4. (Optional) To send a carbon copy to a recipient, enter the name(s) in the **Cc** text box, or double-click the Cc button and enter the name(s) using the Address Book dialog box as explained previously (refer to Figure 7.2).

5. (Optional) If you want to send a blind carbon copy (Bcc) of the message to a recipient, choose View, Bcc Box, which inserts the new field below the **Cc** box. Click the Bcc button to display an address list from which you can select recipients.

6. In the **Subject** entry box, enter the subject, or topic, of this message. After you enter the subject, the title bar on the New Message window changes—it's the same wording as your subject.

ENTERING THE MESSAGE TEXT

After you've filled out all the Header information, you can start typing your message. As soon as you enter text, you'll notice that the formatting toolbar on the message window is no longer greyed out and is now accessible. This is just like using a word processor, and all those toolbar features are available to you. You will learn about them in Lesson 9.

ASSIGNING IMPORTANCE

You can indicate the priority of a message before you send it. This has several uses:

- Recipients who get a lot of e-mail generally read *high*-priority messages first.

- You may want to indicate to a busy recipient that this particular message is of minimal or low importance and it's okay if it's not read immediately.

- When your Microsoft Exchange Server system is very busy, it can be configured to move high-priority messages through the system first.

There are three priority choices: high, normal, and low. Normal is the default and requires no special action. High-priority messages are marked with a red exclamation point in the recipient's Inbox.

Low-priority messages are marked with a blue down arrow. Normal priority messages have no special icons attached to them.

If you want to indicate a high or low priority for a message, follow these steps:

1. In the New Message dialog box, open the View menu and select Toolbar to insert a message window toolbar above the formatting toolbar.

2. Click on the exclamation point button to assign a high priority to this message or click on the down-arrow button to assign a low priority to this message.

SENDING THE MESSAGE

When you have completed your message, it's time to send it. You can send it immediately, or you can specify that you want to send it at a later time.

* To send the message right away, just click on the Send button (or choose File, Send, or press Ctrl+Enter).

* If you want to delay sending the message, choose File, Send Options to display the Send Options dialog box (see Figure 7.3). Choose whether you want the elapsed time before the message is sent to be minutes, hours, days, or weeks, and specify a number.

If you delay sending the message, a copy is placed in the Outbox folder of your mailbox. If you change your mind about sending it, or want to change the Send options, you can delete it.

After the message is sent, a copy is placed in the Sent Items folder of your mailbox.

In this lesson you learned how to compose a message and send it. In the next lesson, you'll learn how to attach items such as files to your messages.

FIGURE 7.3   You can specify the amount of time that elapses
before this message is sent.

ATTACHING ITEMS TO MESSAGES

In this lesson, you'll learn how to attach files or other items to a message. You'll also learn how to access and use attachments that are in messages you receive.

WHAT IS AN ATTACHMENT?

An attachment is a file or an object that is attached to a message. You can place attachments in messages you send, and you can receive messages with attachments.

The usefulness of attachments is unlimited, but the most common reason for attaching a file to a message is to send some information without having to type it into the original message. For example, if you want to send information you received (or wrote) in a word processing document to another member of your organization, you can compose a message that explains that you have this information, perhaps offer some comments on it, and then attach the document in the message so the recipient can read the information.

ATTACHING FILES TO MESSAGES

You can attach an existing file to a message with just a few keystrokes or mouse-clicks. There are a couple of things to be aware of, however, before you try this:

- If the file is a text file (one that does not have specific software codes and can be opened and viewed with any text editor) you can attach the file to any message for any recipient.

- If the file was prepared by a specific software application, the recipient must have access to that software to open and view the file.

First, prepare the message as usual (see Lesson 7 for information on composing a message), then follow these steps:

1. Put your insertion point at the place in the message where you want to insert the icon to indicate the attached file.

2. Choose File, Insert. The Insert File dialog box appears, as shown in Figure 8.1.

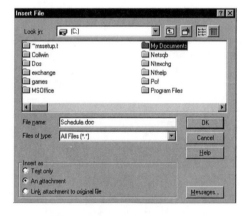

Figure 8.1   Browse your folders to find the document file you want to attach to the message.

3. In the **File name** box of the Insert File dialog box (see Figure 8.1) enter the name of the file you want to insert, or use the **Look in** box to search for the file.

4. In the **Insert as** section at the bottom of the dialog box, select **An attachment**.

5. Click OK. An icon appears in the text area you selected. The document name is under the icon and there is usually a logo or other visual hint in the icon to identify

what software the document was prepared in (see Figure 8.2).

This attachment was created in Microsoft Word.

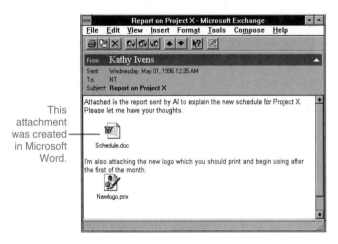

FIGURE 8.2 The icon for the attachment is displayed in your message.

- **TIP** - **Plain Text Attachment** If the attachment you want to send is a plain text file you have two choices for getting the contents to the recipient:

  - You can insert it as an attached file icon into your message, as described earlier.

  - You can insert the text of the file into the message by selecting Text Only in the Insert File dialog box.

RECEIVING AN ATTACHMENT

When a message arrives in your mailbox containing an attachment, a paper clip icon is displayed in the attachment column of your Inbox (see Figure 8.3).

FIGURE 8.3 It's easy to tell when there's a message with an attachment in your mailbox.

Open the message by selecting it and choosing File, Open (or by double-clicking on the message listing). The message, including icons for attachments, is displayed (refer to Figure 8.2).

To open an attachment, double-click on its icon. The associated software starts up and the attachment file is opened. At that point you can use the features of the software to edit, print, or otherwise manipulate the file.

In this lesson you learned about attachments, how to add them to messages you send, and how to view them when you receive messages. In the next lesson, you'll learn more about editing and formatting the text of messages.

EDITING, SPELL CHECKING, AND FORMATTING TEXT

In this lesson, you'll learn how to edit and format the text you enter in your Exchange messages. You'll also learn how to use the Spelling tool.

USING THE EDIT FUNCTIONS

Microsoft Exchange Client provides the standard editing functions you find in most word processors, a spell-checker, and a robust set of features for formatting text. Editing makes working with text easier and faster; spell checking saves embarrassment; and formatting lets you add emphasis, style, and desktop publishing standards to your message.

If you regularly use a Windows-based word processor, you can skip this section because the Edit menu functions in the Exchange message window are the same as those in your word processor. However, if word processing is not part of your daily work, here is an overview of the functions available in the Edit menu:

- **Undo** undoes the last action you performed. For example, if you just accidentally deleted some text, choose Undo to bring it back. Ctrl+Z is a shortcut for Undo.

- **Cut** removes selected (highlighted) text from your message and places it on the Clipboard. Ctrl+X is a shortcut for Cut.

- **Copy** makes a copy of selected text (the text remains in the message) and places it on the Clipboard. Ctrl+C is a shortcut for Copy.

- **Paste** moves the data on the Clipboard into your message, at the insertion point. Ctrl+V is a shortcut for Paste.

- **Find** opens a dialog box in which you can enter specific text you want to look for in your message. For long messages, this is faster than scrolling through the message and looking for the word or phrase you need. Ctrl+Shift+F is a shortcut for Find.

- **Replace** opens a dialog box in which you can enter specific text you want to find. When the text is found, you can change to something else (perhaps you need to find all instances of Smith and replace with Smythe). Ctrl+H is a shortcut for Replace.

Clipboard   A device by which Windows places data into an area of memory and holds it there until you replace it with new data or you exit Windows. Data is placed on the Clipboard by using either the Cut or Copy command from the Edit menu. Clipboard data can be placed in any document prepared in a Windows software application by using Edit, Paste.

USING THE SPELLING TOOL

Exchange provides a spelling tool that you can use to check all the words in your message. The spelling tool looks for a word that is not in its internal dictionary and when it finds one it displays it in the Spelling dialog box.

The spelling tool works in two different ways:

- If you select (highlight) text, it will check that text for spelling errors. This is useful if you've just typed a word and it doesn't look right. After the selected text is checked for spelling, you are asked if you want to check the entire document.

- If you have not selected text, the spelling tool begins checking at your insertion point and moves down through the message. It then returns to the top of the message and works downward until it reaches the original starting point.

Besides the message text, the spelling tool also checks the Subject box in the message header. Attachments are not checked for spelling.

To spell check your messages, follow these steps:

1. Open the message that you want to spell check.

2. Choose Tools, Spelling. The Spelling dialog box is displayed, as shown in Figure 9.1.

FIGURE 9.1 The Spelling dialog box.

3. When the spelling tool displays a word, you have a number of choices:

    - Choose Ignore if you want to skip this specific word.

    - Choose Ignore All if you want to skip this word every time it appears in the text.

    - Choose Add to add the word to the spelling dictionary so the next time you use it, it will be recognized.

- Choose Suggest to display some words that come close to your misspelled word in the **Suggestions** list.

- Choose Change if the suggested word in the **Change To** box is the correct spelling (you can also double-click a word in the suggested word list to change the misspelled word to the correct one).

No Misspelled Words?   The spelling tool only displays the Spelling dialog box if it finds a word that is not in its internal dictionary. Those words may be misspelled or they may just be proper names or technical jargon that are missing from the dictionary. If all the words in your text are in the dictionary, the dialog box never displays and you receive an informational message telling you that the spell check is complete.

4. The spelling tool stops at each misspelled word in your message. When all the text has been checked, an informational message tells you that the spelling check is complete. Click OK to close the spelling tool.

Double Words   The spelling tool also checks for double words, such as "the the." When double words are displayed in the Spelling dialog box, a Delete button replaces the Change button and you can delete one of the words.

Setting Spelling Options

You can configure the way the spelling tool works by configuring the Spelling options. There are three ways to reach the Options dialog box:

- Click the Options button on the Spelling dialog box while it is displaying an unrecognized word.

- Choose Tools, Options in the Message window, then choose the Spelling tab.

- Choose Tools, Options in the Exchange window, then choose the Spelling tab.

With any of these methods, the Spelling options dialog box is displayed as seen in Figure 9.2.

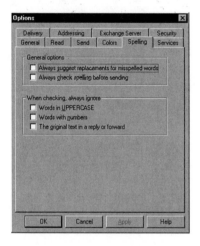

FIGURE 9.2   You can establish Spelling options to suit your own convenience.

Always Suggest   It's probably a good idea to select **Always suggest**, because it saves you the trouble of clicking the Suggest button when you are facing a misspelled word.

Most of the available options should be chosen within the parameters of the type of message you usually send. For example, if you use a lot of acronyms, it's probably wise to configure the speller to ignore **Words in UPPERCASE**.

Formatting Text

You can change the characteristics of your text, or the way specific lines display in your message, with the formatting tools available on the formatting toolbar of the message window (see Figure 9.3).

Figure 9.3 Use the features on the formatting toolbar to enhance your messages.

The features available in the formatting toolbar are easy to understand and are described in Table 9.1.

Table 9.1 Formatting Buttons

Button	Name	Use It To
Arial	Font	Change the font by clicking the arrow to the right of the font box to see a list of available fonts, then select the one you want to use
10	Font size	Change the font size by clicking the arrow to the right of the font size box and selecting the one you want to use
B	Bold	Turn bold on and off
I	Italic	Turn italic on and off
U	Underline	Turn underline on and off

Button	Name	Use It To
	Color text	Change the color of the displayed text (and printed text, if you have a color printer) by selecting a color from the list that displays when you click this button
	Bullets	Place a bullet at the beginning of each paragraph
	Decrease Indent	Decrease the indentation of a paragraph by one tab stop
	Increase Indent	Increase the indentation of a paragraph by one tab stop
	Align Left	Line text up on the left with jagged right edges
	Center	Center each line of text between the margins
	Align Right	Line text up on the right with jagged left edges

You can add formatting as you type, or after you've completed entering text:

- If you want to add formatting as you go, select the appropriate formatting button, then begin entering text. The buttons are toggles, so that when you want to end a particular formatting style, just click the button again to turn it off.

- If you want to format existing text, select (highlight) the text and click the appropriate formatting button.

TIP **Formatting Options** You can choose multiple formatting options, such as Bold and Italic, Underline and Cen-
ter, or any other combination.

 When to Avoid Formatting The formatting features
supplied with Exchange Client are called Rich Text Formatting (RTF). If your message is going to a recipient on
the Internet, CompuServe, or one of the other online services, you cannot use RTF formatting because it is not
supported by these services.

In this lesson you learned about the editing and formatting tools
and the spell-check feature of Microsoft Exchange Client. In the
next lesson you'll learn about the options you have when receiving messages.

RECEIVING MESSAGES

In this lesson, you'll learn how to open messages you've received from others and work with them. This includes replying to the sender, forwarding to another recipient, and printing copies of the message.

OPENING MESSAGES

Your received mail is stored in the Inbox of your mailbox, and you can see the list of messages in the contents pane by selecting the Inbox object in the folder pane (see Lesson 2 for a discussion about the mailbox display).

When you see the list of messages in the contents pane, the header information helps you decide which messages to read immediately and which messages can wait. You can use the priority icons, the subject matter, or just pick messages sent by people you like to hear from.

Scroll through the list to find the message you want to open. Then double-click on it, and the message opens in a message window (see Figure 10.1).

The buttons on the message window toolbar provide quick access to many of the available options for working with received messages. Table 10.1 lists the toolbar buttons and their functions.

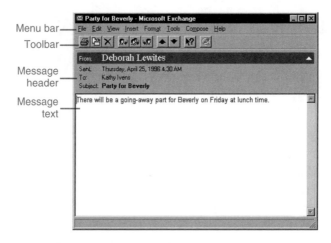

Menu bar

Toolbar

Message
header

Message
text

FIGURE 10.1 The text of the message displays, and the
message window provides tools for working with the message.

**TABLE 10.1 TOOLBAR BUTTONS FOR WORKING WITH RECEIVED
MESSAGES**

BUTTON	NAME	FUNCTION
	Print	Prints the message
	Move	Moves the message to a folder you choose
	Delete	Deletes the message
	Reply to Sender	Opens a new message window with the sender's name in the To box
	Reply to All	Opens a new message window with all recipients of the current message indicated as recipients of the new message
	Forward	Sends this message to another recipient

BUTTON	NAME	FUNCTION
▲	Previous	Opens the message immediately above the current message in the contents pane
▼	Next	Opens the message immediately below the current message in the contents pane
▶?	Help	Displays information about specific elements in the received message window
🖉	Read digital signature	If advanced security is enabled, displays information about the password-protected signature of the sender

REPLYING TO MESSAGES

Frequently you'll want to reply to the message you've just read. The sender may have asked a question that requires an answer from you, you may want to make a comment about the contents, or you may just want to acknowledge that you received the message.

To compose a reply to the person who sent you the message, follow these steps:

1. Click the Reply to Sender button, which opens a new message window that is already set up to reply to the message you just read (see Figure 10.2).

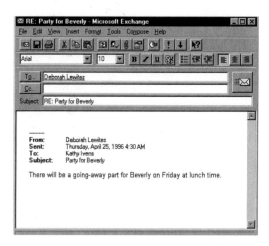

FIGURE 10.2   The message window for composing a reply.

 Reply to All Recipients If the original message was sent to multiple recipients (you may even have been a carbon copy recipient), and you want to reply to everyone who received the original message, click the Reply to All button instead of the Reply to Sender button. Every recipient's name is automatically added to the message header.

2. Start typing at the insertion point, which is above the original message (the original message is indented and a line appears above it, to separate it from your reply). Here are some additional options from which to choose:

- If you prefer, you can move the insertion point below the original message to have your reply follow it.

- If you don't think the original message is needed to understand your reply, you can delete it.

- You can insert additional recipients in the **To** or **Cc** box if you want to send this reply message to others.

- You can change the text in the Subject box to reflect the contents of your reply more accurately.

- You can use all the formatting features as you enter your reply.

3. Click the Send button when you have finished composing your reply.

INCLUDING THE ORIGINAL MESSAGE IN YOUR REPLY

By default, the original message text is inserted in the reply. It is indented to make it stand out. This can be helpful if you want to enter comments or notes within the original message's text.

If you find that most of the time you don't need to keep the original message text in your reply (and you constantly have to take the trouble to delete it) you can change the default setup so that the original text is not automatically placed in the message section of your reply. To do this, follow these steps:

1. Choose Tools, Options to display the Options dialog box.

2. Click on the Read tab (see Figure 10.3).

3. Deselect (click to remove the check mark) the option to **Include the original text when replying**.

4. Deselect **Indent the original text when replying**, to change the original message's position in your reply so that it starts at the left margin (if you are opting to keep the original text).

5. Deselect **Close the original item** if you want to keep the original message window open while you are composing your reply.

6. Click the Font button to see a list of available fonts, and choose a new default font for all your reply messages.

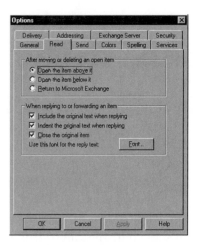

FIGURE 10.3   You can alter the default behavior for replying to a message.

7. When you complete your changes, click OK to return to the Reply Message window, or click Cancel to undo your changes.

TIP   **Keep the Original Message Open**   If you decide you don't want to have the original text placed in your reply, there can be an advantage to deselecting the option to close the original item. If you want to check the text in the original message—just drag your reply window off to the side to see the original message behind it.

FORWARDING MESSAGES

Sometimes you receive information in a message that you think might be of interest to someone else (someone who was not sent a copy of the message). When this happens, you can forward the message, which means the original message is sent to a new recipient. You can add your own text to the original contents if you want to. To forward a received message, follow these steps:

1. With the received message open, click the Forward button to open a new message window as seen in Figure 10.4.

FIGURE 10.4   When you forward a message, the Subject box includes a notation that indicates that fact.

2. Enter a recipient (or multiple recipients) in the **To** box. You can also send carbon copies to as many recipients as you want to.

3. Move your pointer into the text area to add your own comments.

4. Click on Send when you are ready to send the message.

Attachments Are Forwarded Too   When you forward a message that has an attachment, the attachment is copied into the forwarded message.

Printing Messages

There might be times when you need a printed copy of a message, either to study it more carefully or to file it. You can print any message whether you have opened it or not:

- If the message is open, click the Print button on the message window's toolbar.

- If the message is not open, select its listing in the contents pane and click the Print button on the Exchange Client window's toolbar.

If you use the Print button, the message is sent to the printer immediately—no Print dialog box appears to enable you to change the printer or any other print setup configuration.

If you have to change printers or make any other adjustments to the printing process (perhaps you want to print multiple copies), you must choose File, Print or press Ctrl+P to display the Print dialog box.

TIP   **Printing Attachments**   By default, attachments don't print when you print a message—only the message text is sent to the printer. If you want to print the attachment, you must open the Print dialog box and select the option to **Print attachments**.

In this lesson, you learned how to open a received message and perform several operations on it—replying, forwarding, and printing. In the next lesson you'll learn some of the ways you can manage the storage and handling of messages.

Managing Messages

In this lesson, you'll learn how to manage the messages you receive. You'll learn how to create folders to store messages, how to delete messages, and how to rescue deleted messages.

Storing Messages

After you open and read a received message, and then close it, the message stays in the Inbox—you know it's been read because its listing is no longer displayed in bold type. Some of those old messages can be deleted, but there are many you'll want to save for future reference. There are many options available for storing messages.

If you delete the message, it's sent to the Deleted Items folder in your mailbox. The options for manipulating the Deleted Items folder is discussed later in this lesson.

If you want to store messages you've already read, you can create a filing system for them by creating folders that enable you to sort the messages by whatever system suits your needs.

There are two types of folders you can create to hold the messages you want to save:

- Mailbox folders, which you create with names that match your storage scheme. These folders are part of your mailbox and are displayed in the contents pane when you select your mailbox in the folders pane, along with the four folders already attached to your mailbox. Mailbox folders are stored on the server, because they are part of your mailbox.

- Personal folders, which are additional folders you can

create for yourself. They display in the folder pane of your Microsoft Exchange Client window and can be stored on your local hard drive. See Lesson 13 for information on creating and using personal folders.

CREATING AND USING MAILBOX FOLDERS

You can create folders to hold specific types of messages and keep those folders in your mailbox. You may, for example, want to keep messages about a specific project all together in one folder. Or, use one folder for all the information that arrives about your employee benefits, employee records, and other administrative messages about your organization.

While mailbox folders make it easy to find old messages, there is one thing you have to be careful about—the amount of room these folders can take up on the server. In some organizations, the space reserved for your mailbox may be limited by the administrators to conserve disk space on the server. If this is the case, you'll want to use mailbox folders judiciously and create personal folders on your local hard drive for the messages you want to save.

TIP   **Holding Folders**   One of the best ways to use mailbox folders is as a temporary holding bin until you can decide where to store a message permanently. This also is a good place to store any message that needs a reply from you (but not an instant reply, which you would have done while the message was open).

To create a new folder for your mailbox, follow these steps:

1. In the folder pane, select your mailbox. The contents pane lists the four default mailbox folders (**Deleted Items, Inbox, Outbox, Sent Items**).

2. Choose File, New Folder to display the New Folder dialog box (see Figure 11.1).

FIGURE 11.1   The New Folder dialog box creates a folder at the location of the selected item in the folder pane.

3. Name the folder, then click OK.

The new folder appears in the contents pane when your mailbox is selected (see Figure 11.2).

FIGURE 11.2   The new folder is displayed with the other mailbox folders, in its correct alphabetic placement.

USING MAILBOX FOLDERS

After your new mailbox folder has been created, it's easy to place messages into it. You can either move or copy a message into a mailbox folder, and you can perform either of those actions on both open or closed messages.

WORKING WITH CLOSED MESSAGES

The easiest way to put a message into a mailbox folder is to work with a closed message, because you can simply drag the message from the list in the contents panel into the folder. To accomplish this, follow these easy steps:

1. Make sure the mailbox folders are displayed in the folder pane (click the plus sign next to the mailbox).

2. Select the Inbox folder in the folder pane to display all your received messages in the contents pane, as shown in Figure 11.3.

Display the mailbox folders

Click the Inbox folder to display mail messages

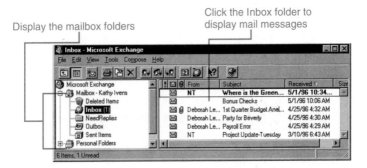

Figure 11.3 If the messages and the folders are both displayed, it's easy to drag messages to the folder of your choice.

3. To move a message to a mailbox folder, drag it to the folder's icon.

4. To copy a message to a mailbox folder, hold down Ctrl while you drag it to the folder's icon.

Working with Multiple Messages To move or copy multiple messages, select them (hold down the Ctrl key while you select each one), then drag any one to the target folder—the others come along.

Working with Open Messages

To place a message (or a copy of a message) in a mailbox folder when the message is open, follow these steps:

1. Choose File, Move or File, Copy.

2. When the Move or Copy dialog box displays (they are both the same), click on the plus sign next to the Mailbox object to display the mailbox folders (see Figure 11.4).

Figure 11.4   The Move and Copy dialog boxes display the objects in your folders pane.

3. Click the folder into which you want to move or copy the current open message, then click OK.

Deleting Messages

Similarly to moving or copying, you can delete a message whether it is open or closed. Deleted messages are moved to the Deleted Items folder in your mailbox. You can delete a message by using any of the following methods:

- Delete an open message by clicking the Delete button on the toolbar.

• Delete a closed message by selecting it, then pressing Del (or dragging it to the Deleted Items folder in the folder pane).

TIP   **Deleting Multiple Messages**   You can select multiple messages from the list in the contents pane by holding down Ctrl while you click on each message you want to delete. Press Del to delete all the selected messages.

RETRIEVING DELETED MESSAGES

If you accidently delete a message you need, you can retrieve it from the Deleted Items folder with these steps:

1. Select the Deleted Items folder in the folder pane. This displays a list of its contents in the contents pane.

2. Select the message you want to retrieve in the contents pane.

3. Choose File, Move.

4. When the Move dialog box appears, choose the target folder you need (usually the Inbox).

UNDERSTANDING AUTOMATIC DELETION

The default configuration for Exchange is to move deleted messages into the Deleted Items folder and keep them there as long as you are working in the Exchange software. When you exit Exchange, the messages in the Deleted Items folder are removed permanently and cannot be recovered.

You can change this to have the Deleted Items folder continue to hold deleted messages until you specifically remove them. To change this configuration, follow these steps:

1. Choose Tools, Options to bring up the Options dialog box with the General properties tab in the foreground (see Figure 11.5).

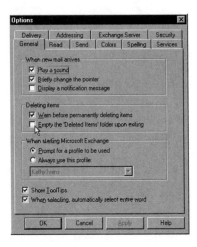

FIGURE 11.5   You can change your configuration to hold deleted messages until you're ready to delete them yourself.

2. Deselect **Empty the 'Deleted Items' folder upon exiting**, by clicking on the box next to the item.

3. Click OK.

PERMANENTLY DELETING MESSAGES

If you choose to keep deleted messages after you exit Microsoft Exchange Client, eventually your Deleted Items folder will take up quite a bit of disk space. You should examine and empty your Deleted Items folder on a regular basis, perhaps weekly.

- Delete individual messages by selecting the Deleted Items folder in the folder pane and selecting the messages you can safely get rid of in the contents pane. Then press Del.

- Delete all the messages contained in the Deleted Items folder by clicking on the Deleted Items object with the

right mouse button, then choose Empty folder from the
context menu.

 If you're using Windows 3.x you don't have right mouse
button functions, and you will have to select the messages (Ctrl+A selects all messages) and then delete
them.

In this lesson you learned how to manage your messages, and
how Microsoft Exchange Client deletes messages. In the next
lesson you'll learn about faxing with Exchange.

WORKING WITH FAXES— FOR WINDOWS 95 CLIENTS

12

In this lesson, you'll learn how to use the Windows 95 Microsoft Exchange Client to create a fax and send it. You'll also learn about some of the options available for sending and receiving faxes.

When Microsoft Exchange Client is installed on your workstation, you can use it for faxing instead of turning to the fax program that is part of the accessories package that came with your operating system.

If you don't have a modem, or network access to a shared modem, you probably don't have fax services installed in your Exchange system (either ask your administrator about gaining fax services or skip this lesson).

COMPOSING A FAX IN EXCHANGE

To send a fax, choose Compose, New Fax to start the Compose New Fax Wizard (see Figure 12.1) and then follow these steps:

1. Assuming you fax from your office computer, your location information is pre-set. Just choose Next on the Fax Wizard page to move on.

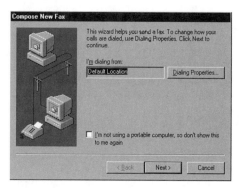

FIGURE 12.1   The Fax Wizard walks you through the process of sending a fax.

 TIP   **Locations**   You can configure multiple location settings if you use fax services from various locations. For example, if you travel you might have a location setting that dials special numbers to get an outside line (as you would do from a hotel). If you only fax from your office and the settings never change, select I'm not using a portable computer so you can skip the Locations page of the Wizard.

2. On the next Wizard page enter the name of the recipient in the **To** box (see Figure 12.2), and also enter the phone number. If the recipient is in your Address Book, click on the Address Book button and choose an address list, then choose a recipient. If the recipient is not in the Address Book, you can choose New to add this recipient to the Address Book. Click on Next when you are finished.

3. The next Wizard page asks if you want to use a cover page and also gives you the opportunity to change the default options for sending faxes. These options permit you to send the fax at a later time, and include security (encryption) options. Click on Options to configure these items, then choose OK to return to the Wizard page. Choose Next when you have finished this page of the Fax Wizard.

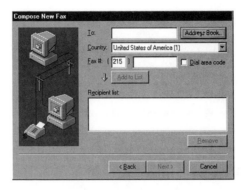

FIGURE 12.2 The recipient and phone number have to be entered in the Fax Wizard.

4. Fill in the **Subject** text and then enter text in the **Note** section. (If you are using a cover page, you will have an option button that allows you to begin the text on the cover page instead of starting a new page.) Choose Next.

5. If you want to attach a file to your fax, choose Add File on this Wizard page. Enter the file name in the **Files to send** box. Choose Next.

Attaching Files You can only attach files to your fax if the fax recipient uses a computer to receive faxes, and has software that can open the attached document.

6. The final Wizard page informs you that you have completed all the steps for composing and sending a fax. Choose Finish to send the fax (or, if you opted for later transmission, this will store the fax until it is time to send it).

Sending Faxes

Whether you send your fax immediately after it's composed or at a later time, the process of sending a fax is the same. All the steps are performed automatically and the Microsoft Fax Status dialog box reports each step of the process (preparing the fax format, dialing the number, and sending the pages). The Sent Items folder in your mailbox shows your fax in its list.

Setting Options for Sending Faxes

You can configure the default options for sending fax transmissions so that you can take advantage of lower phone line rates, or set a specific time for sending all your faxes. (This is helpful if you're sharing a modem.)

To configure your fax sending options, follow these steps:

1. Open the Tools menu and place the pointer on Microsoft Fax Tools to display the submenu.

2. From the submenu, choose Options to bring up the Microsoft Fax Properties dialog box, with the Message tab in the foreground (see Figure 12.3).

3. Use the following options for sending faxes:

    - Choose As soon as possible if you customarily send a fax as soon as you've finished preparing it.

    - If you usually send faxes over long-distance lines, choose Discount rates, then choose Set. The Set Discount Rates dialog box appears (see Figure 12.4). Set the **Start** and **End** times of your long-distance carrier's discount period and click OK to return to the Fax Modems Properties dialog box.

    - To set a time for sending faxes, choose Specific time, then enter the time.

•You also can establish other configuration options on this tab, including message formats, default cover pages, and whether you can change the subject line for received faxes.

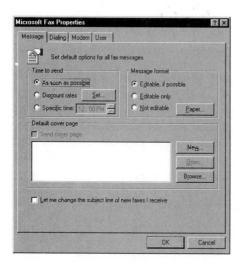

FIGURE 12.3   Choose a default method for sending faxes—you can change the default for any individual fax.

FIGURE 12.4   You can specify the hours during which long-distance rates are less expensive to save money sending long-distance faxes.

4. When you've finished, click OK to return to the Exchange mailbox.

RECEIVING FAXES

Depending on your configuration options (usually established when fax services were installed), there are several ways in which your modem can respond when someone sends you a fax:

- The modem automatically answers an incoming call

- The modem never answers a call unless you force it to

- A dialog box displays to ask if you want the modem to answer

By default, Exchange chooses the option to not answer calls. If you have a modem attached to your computer, you'll probably want to change that option so you can receive faxes. (If faxes for you are received by a network modem, they're placed in your Inbox the same way e-mail that arrives for you is placed there.)

TELLING THE MODEM WHETHER TO ANSWER

To set the configuration for the modem's behavior, follow these steps:

1. Open the Tools menu, place the pointer on the Microsoft Fax Tools entry, and select Options from the submenu.

2. Choose the Modem tab.

3. Select your fax modem, then choose Properties to display the Fax Modem Properties dialog box (see Figure 12.5).

4. Choose from one of the following answer modes:

    - Select Answer after, then specify the number of rings, to have the modem answer the phone at that point. This is useful if you share the modem with your voice line (and generally manage to say "hello" before the number of rings you specify for modem answering).

    - Choose Manual to tell the modem when to answer

the phone. This is useful if people generally call you to tell you they're sending you a fax. (See the next section of this lesson for more information.)

- Choose Don't answer if you don't want the modem to answer the phone automatically. There is a way to answer if you know a fax is arriving, which is explained in the next section.

5. After you select your option, click OK to return to the Microsoft Fax Properties dialog box. Click OK again to return to the Exchange mailbox.

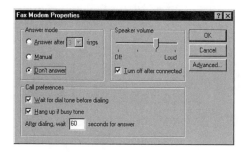

FIGURE 12.5   Reconfigure Answer mode to have your modem answer the phone for incoming faxes.

MANUALLY ANSWERING THE PHONE

If you choose Manual or Don't Answer as the configuration option, you can control whether to have the modem answer the phone each time it rings. If you know a fax is arriving, it does, otherwise, it doesn't.

For the Manual answering configuration, when the phone rings, an information dialog box displays asking if you want to receive a fax (see Figure 12.6).

For the Don't Answer configuration, when the phone rings and you know it's a fax, click the fax machine icon on the right side of the taskbar (next to the clock). The Fax Status dialog box displays (see Figure 12.7) and you can choose Answer Now to force the modem to receive the fax.

FIGURE 12.6   The modem knows the phone is ringing and wants to know if you want to answer it.

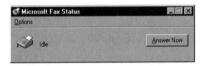

FIGURE 12.7   Open the Fax Status dialog box from the taskbar icon to tell the modem to answer the phone.

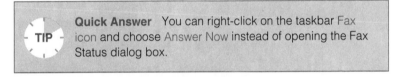

Quick Answer   You can right-click on the taskbar Fax icon and choose Answer Now instead of opening the Fax Status dialog box.

VIEWING THE FAX

After the modem answers the phone and receives the fax, it's placed in your Inbox. There's a Fax icon in the Message Type column so you can tell it's not a regular e-mail message. Often, there's no data available for the **From** or **Subject** columns.

Double-click on the fax listing to open the Fax Viewer and read the fax message. (If you receive a fax from another Microsoft Exchange Client user, you can treat it as a regular e-mail message and the usual message window opens rather than the Fax Viewer.)

Faxes that are sent from free-standing fax machines can sometimes be difficult to read. Frequently, senders put the fax in upside down or it goes through the machine at an extremely crooked angle. Instead of standing on your head or tilting way over, use the tools on the Fax Viewer to rotate the fax as needed.

You also can zoom in when the font is too small to read. The tools on the Fax Viewer are easy to use and are self-explanatory (or click on Help if you need it).

In this lesson you learned how you can compose, send, receive and read faxes from a Windows 95 Microsoft Exchange Client system. In the next lesson, you'll learn how to create and use personal folders.

USING PERSONAL FOLDERS

In this lesson, you'll learn how to create, configure, and use personal folders to store messages and files.

Personal folders are useful for storing file s and messages you want to keep for your own use. You can collect information from many sources and store it in one place, or store it in multiple personal folders according to a category sorting scheme that is easy to work with.

Personal folders are usually stored on your own hard drive, although you can store them on the server (which reduces the privacy of the folders).

The capability to have personal folders is not automatic. This feature must be added to your Microsoft Exchange Client profile. If this feature has already been established, there is a Personal Folders object in the folders pane of your Exchange window. If that object doesn't exist, you will have to add the feature to your profile (see your system administrator). This lesson assumes you have the capability to add personal folders to your system.

CREATING A PERSONAL FOLDER

The Personal Folder object that appears in your viewer is the container into which you place all the personal folders you create. There is a plus sign (+) next to the object, indicating there are subfolders in this container. By default, there is a Deleted Items personal folder which provides the same service as the Deleted Items folder in your mailbox—to hold deleted items so you can either retrieve them or delete them permanently. See Lesson 11 for information about the mailbox Deleted Items folder.

You can create as many personal folders as you need by following these steps:

1. Select (highlight) the Personal Folder object, then choose File, New Folder. The New Folder dialog box appears, as shown in Figure 13.1.

2. In the New Folder dialog box, enter a name for the folder, then click OK.

FIGURE 13.1   The name for a personal folder should indicate the items it will hold.

 TIP   **Nested Personal Folders**   You can create personal subfolders under any personal folder if you want to maintain files and messages in a sorting scheme that requires it. Just select the parent folder and create the new folder while the parent folder is highlighted.

USING PERSONAL FOLDERS

After you create a personal folder, it's easy to place items into it. For example, you can:

- Put received messages or attachments into a personal folder by highlighting the item and choosing Copy or Move, then choosing the personal folder as the target.

- Add files to a personal folder by opening Explorer while the Microsoft Exchange Client viewer is open. Drag the file from its original directory to the folder. (This system works in Windows 95 and Windows NT 4.0.)

- Copy or move items from one personal folder to another.

- If you have the necessary rights and permissions, copy items from a public folder into a personal folder. (See Lesson 14 for information about public folders.)

To view or manipulate any item in a personal folder, just select that personal folder in the folders pane and the items stored in the folder are displayed in the contents pane. Double-click on the item of interest to open it.

MANAGING PERSONAL FOLDERS

You have some configuration decisions and management functions for your personal folders that you might want to exercise. For example:

- You can change the name of your personal folders services in Microsoft Exchange Client (which also changes the name of the Personal Folder object in your viewer).

- You can password-protect your personal folders (useful if you store them on the server or if other people share the use of your computer).

- You can compact your Personal Folders file (get rid of blank spaces as a result of deletions) to save disk space.

To exercise these options, follow these steps:

1. Choose Tools, Services to display the Services dialog box.

2. Select Personal Folders, then choose Properties. The Personal Folders dialog box appears (see Figure 13.2).

3. As discussed previously, you can change the **Name**, add a **Comment**, add or **Change Password**, or compact the folder file. (See the sections that follow for more information about setting passwords and compacting personal folders.)

4. Click OK to complete the configuration process.

FIGURE 13.2   You can configure the properties of your personal folders services in the Personal Folders dialog box.

The two important choices in the dialog box are the password feature and the compaction utility.

While Microsoft Exchange Client gives you the opportunity to change the name of your personal folders services, it's usually not necessary.

And, the capability to add comments to your personal folder configuration isn't important to the way the personal folder feature works, but you may think of some note you want to write to yourself about your personal folders and you can use the **Comment** text box to do so.

PASSWORD PROTECTION

When you password protect your personal folders, you are not applying a password to any specific personal folder; you are applying a password to the file that holds all your personal folders. To add a password to your personal folders, follow these steps:

1. From the Personal Folders properties dialog box, choose Change Password to display the Change Password dialog box seen in Figure 13.3.

2. Enter the **Old password** if there is one, otherwise, press Tab to move to the next field.

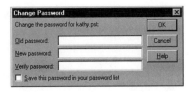

FIGURE 13.3   When you enter text in this dialog box, you won't see it. It's a secret, so you'll only see stars (****).

3. Type in the **New password**. Then press Tab to move to the next field.

4. Retype the new password in the **Verify Password** box— if the characters don't match the new password, you'll be able to reenter both the new password and the verify entry.

5. Select **Save this password in your password list**, if you don't want to type the password each time you use your personal folders.

6. Click OK when you are finished.

TIP   **Save Password**   If you choose **Save this password**, your new password is stored in a password list and you won't be asked to enter it when you access your personal folders file. However, if someone with a different name is logged on to your computer, or if another user attempts to access your personal folder file from a different computer on the network, the password will be requested.

COMPACTING THE PERSONAL FOLDER FILE

Every time you add a new personal folder, or place a message or file into a personal folder, the file that holds the personal folders gets bigger. When you delete an item, or move an item somewhere else on your system, the file doesn't shrink itself even though there's less in it. That means as you add more and more items, and continue to delete items, the file simply gets larger because of the additions and the empty space left by the deleted files.

You can compact the personal folder file so that it gets rid of the blank spots and reduces itself to the size needed to hold the current contents. Of course, as you add new items, it grows again, and it continues to leave behind blank spots when you delete items—so you'll have to compact it from time to time.

To compact the personal folder file, click on Compact Now on the Personal Folders dialog box. An informational dialog box appears to let you know that the process is under way, and gives you a chance to Cancel if you want to (see Figure 13.4). Compacting can take a few seconds or a few minutes, depending on how many items you have in personal folders.

FIGURE 13.4   Compact your personal folders file to save disk space.

In this lesson you learned how to create and manage personal folders. In the next lesson, you'll learn about public folders, what they are, and how you can use them.

14

Using Public Folders

In this lesson, you'll learn about public folders—what they are and how to use them.

Public folders are used to store items (files, company forms, or any other information) that can be accessed by all the users on your Microsoft Exchange Server system. Public folders are created at workstations, by users, but they are stored on the server. (Personal folders, covered in Lesson 13, are kept on the user's local hard drive.)

Understanding Public Folders

Public folders make it easy to distribute information to everyone in the organization. An item can be placed in a folder instead of being sent through e-mail to a long list of users. It's a simple way to let everyone read an interesting text file about some topic important to the company's well-being, distribute the latest company employee handbook, circulate general announcements about company policies or company events, or distribute items to those employees who are working together on a project.

Each server in your Microsoft Exchange Server system holds the public folders that have been created by the users attached to that server. Then, at regular periods during each day, the public folders and their contents are replicated to all the other servers in the organization. This way, every user can have access to every folder regardless of the folder's origination point.

When you see the display of public folders in your Microsoft Exchange Client window, you can't tell the difference between public folders that were created on the server on your site, and public folders that were created at other, remote servers and replicated onto your own server. But, it doesn't matter, because the replication function ensures that there is a copy of every public folder on the server to which you're attached.

By default, no user of Microsoft Exchange Client is permitted to create a public folder. An administrator must either make specific configuration changes to Microsoft Exchange Server to permit the creation of public folders at certain workstations, or create the public folders at the administrator's own workstation. This lesson assumes that someone was given the necessary rights to create them, and there are some public folders in your system.

When you look at the display in the folders pane of your Microsoft Exchange Client window, the top level of public folders is a container folder named Public Folders (see Figure 14.1). Under that folder is a subfolder named All Public Folders, which contains all the public folders for the system. There also may be a Favorites folder displayed. (Information about the Favorites folder is found in Lesson 16.)

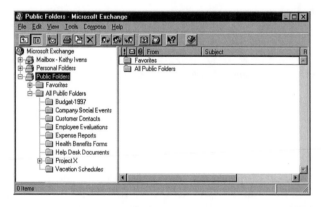

FIGURE 14.1   The public folders are displayed in a hierarchy that starts with a Public Folder container.

Container Folder   A folder that is designed specifically to hold other folders is a container folder. The icon for a container folder differs from that of a regular folder—it depicts a folder sitting in a box.

CHECKING ACCESS PERMISSIONS TO PUBLIC FOLDERS

To open a public folder and view its contents, you must have the necessary permissions for reading a public folder. Likewise, you must have the necessary permissions if you want to add items to a public folder. Companywide folders are usually created with these rights for every user. Project folders or folders created for specific uses give rights to the appropriate user list.

Permissions   In Microsoft Exchange Server, permissions are the spelling out of the tasks you are permitted to perform, such as read, or write permissions. Roles have been established that are specific combinations of permissions.

UNDERSTANDING ROLES

Roles are combinations of rights. Various combinations of rights have been put together and assigned a name by Microsoft Exchange Server, and you can choose whatever role has the combination you prefer to give to a delegate. Here are the predefined roles and their attendant rights:

- Owners have all permissions.
- Publishing Editors can create, read, edit, and delete items and create subfolders.

- Editors can create, read, edit, and delete items.

- Publishing Authors can create and read items; edit and delete the items they create and create subfolders.

- Authors can create and read items and edit and delete the items they create.

- Reviewers can read items.

- Contributors can create items.

When you select a role, the rights for that role are selected automatically in the Permissions section of the dialog box. If you select an additional right, or deselect a given right (or both), a role that matches the new permissions configuration is automatically chosen.

If you choose a combination of permissions that does not match a defined role, the role will be named Custom.

To see if you have permission to access a public folder, right-click on the folder and choose Properties from the context menu to display the folder's Properties dialog box (see Figure 14.2).

FIGURE 14.2   A Properties dialog box for a public folder.

Your role, and the permissions attached to that role, are displayed in the Properties dialog box of each public folder. The dialog box also displays the name of the public folder's owner. You can contact that person to get additional permissions.

VIEWING AND WORKING WITH PUBLIC FOLDER CONTENTS

To view the items in a public folder, select that folder in the folder pane to display its contents in the contents pane (see Figure 14.3).

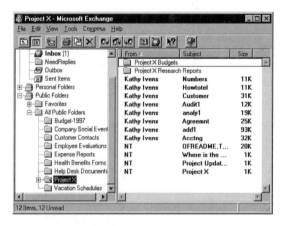

FIGURE 14.3   All the items contained in the public folder are displayed in the contents pane.

To manipulate any of the items in a public folder, right-click on the item to bring up the context menu (see Figure 14.4).

 TIP   **Quick Open**   The context menu choice of Open is the default action, so if you want to open an item, just double-click on it instead of right-clicking and then choosing Open.

FIGURE 14.4   The context menu lists all the operations you can perform on an item.

Working with public folder items isn't much different from working with messages or files from software applications:

- **Open**   The software that was used to prepare the item launches, and the item is displayed in the software window. If the item is a standard message, the message is displayed in the Exchange message window.

- **SaveAs**   Saves the item in a different location. The SaveAs dialog box displays so you can choose a location, a file name, and a file type.

- **Move**   Moves the item out of the current folder and into a different folder in your Microsoft Exchange Client system.

- **Copy**   Copies the item to another folder in your Microsoft Exchange Client system.

- **Print**   Prints the item.

- **Reply to Sender**   For a message, opens a message window so you can send a reply to the sender.

- **Post Reply in This Folder**   Used to respond to a message that requires a specific form.

- **Forward**   For a message, sends a copy to another user.

- **Delete**   Deletes the item (if you have the correct permissions).

- **Properties**   Displays the properties of the item.

 Form   A document created and used in Microsoft Exchange Server for a specific purpose. Forms are attached to specific public folders and are used to limit the way items are placed in a public folder. An example of a form is a vacation schedule, an expense report, or any other document that requires you to fill out a preconfigured form instead of entering data.

ADDING ITEMS TO PUBLIC FOLDERS

If you have permission to post to a public folder, you can add an item, either by copying the item from another folder in your Microsoft Exchange Client system, or by copying a file created in a software application.

Copying a file from your general file system is a bit tricky, because your Microsoft Exchange Client folders aren't listed in File Manager or Explorer (because they aren't regular directories/folders). To add a file from your computer file system to an Exchange folder, follow these steps:

1. Open File Manager or Explorer (depending on the operating system you're using).

2. Arrange your screen so that you can see both the Microsoft Exchange Client viewer and File Manager (or Explorer).

3. Drag the file from File Manager or Explorer to the appropriate folder in the folder pane of the Exchange viewer (hold down Ctrl while dragging to copy the file instead of moving it).

The method in which public folders are implemented, the permissions given to users, and the forms created for individual public folders are all a reflection of the policies and philosophies of your organization. No two companies implement this feature the same way. Your access to public folders will match the manner in which public folders are adapted at your company.

In this lesson you learned about public folders, and how to access them and manipulate their contents. The next lesson discusses the administration of public folders.

15

L E S S O N

ADMINISTERING PUBLIC FOLDERS

In this lesson, you'll learn how to perform some of the available administative tasks on a public folder you've created.

If the system administrator has given you permission to create public folders, any folder you create has your name on it as the owner. The owner has all rights and permissions to a public folder, can establish permissions for other users, and controls the way contents are displayed in the folder.

SETTING PUBLIC FOLDER PERMISSIONS

As the owner of a public folder, you have the ability to decide which users have rights to access the folder, and what the extent of those rights are.

To configure permissions for a public folder you own, right-click on the folder and choose Properties from the context menu. In the Properties dialog box, click on the Permissions tab.

Figure 15.1 shows the Properties dialog box (with the Permissions tab in the foreground) as it appears to the owner.

When You're Not the Owner You might want to take a quick peek at Figure 14.2 in Lesson 14 to see the way a Properties dialog box displays a folder that you don't own—there are fewer tabs displayed because you have fewer rights.

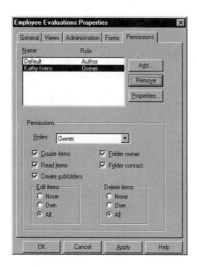

FIGURE 15.1   Use the Permissions tab to give rights for this folder to other users.

By default, all users can access public folders with the role of Author (read and create items, enabling users to see the information posted to the folder and to post their own items to the folder).

You can change the default role, and you can add users and give them specific rights. To add users and assign rights, follow these steps:

1. On the **Permissions** tab, choose Add to display a list of users, then double-click on the user you want to add. Click OK.

2. When the user's name appears on the Permissions tab, the default role is selected. To change the role, click on the name to highlight it, then click on the arrow to the right of the **Roles** box and select a Role for this user (see Figure 15.2).

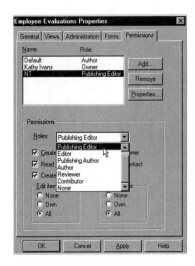

FIGURE 15.2   Choose a role for the user you are currently working on for permissions.

Change the Default Role   If you want to change the default role for users, highlight that entry and pick another role. If you want to keep out all users except those you specifically designate, you can choose a default role of None.

UNDERSTANDING ROLES

A *role* is a predefined set of rights. When you choose a role for a user, you're actually choosing a specific list of rights. After the rights are selected (displayed with a check mark), you can select additional rights, or deselect any rights. If the changes you make match the rights assigned to another role, the name of that role will be displayed. If the changes you make create a set of rights that don't match any existing role, the name of the role that displays will be "custom."

CHANGING THE FOLDER'S VIEW

A *view* is the way the information in a folder is displayed when users open the folder. It is a specific combination of columns, categories, and sort order. You can change any of those items to have some control over what is seen, and how it is ordered.

To configure a view for a public folder, follow these steps:

1. Click the View tab of the folder's Properties dialog box (see Figure 15.3).

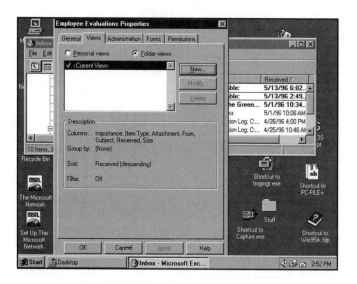

FIGURE 15.3   All the details about a highlighted view are displayed.

2. Choose New to create a new set of criteria for viewing the contents of the folder.

3. In the New View dialog box (see Figure 15.4), set up the conditions for displaying the folder's contents.

FIGURE 15.4 Use the New View dialog box to design the criteria that controls what users see when they open this folder.

4. Enter a name for this view in the **View name** box.

5. Choose Columns to display the Columns dialog box (see Figure 15.5). Add and remove columns by selecting them in the **Available columns** list and clicking either Add or Remove. Columns that have been added can be moved up or down (which means left and right on the actual folder display). Click OK to return to the New View dialog box.

6. Choose Group by if you want to organize the display of the folder's contents in related groups. The Group By dialog box lets you group contents according to the column categories you've selected. Within each group you can sort (ascending or descending) by any column category.

7. Choose Sort to sort the contents by one of the selected column categories. Use Sort if you didn't use Group (grouped contents are already sorted).

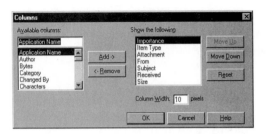

FIGURE 15.5 Highlight a column, then Add or Remove it.

8. Choose Filter to establish a set of rules that will include or exclude the display of items in this folder (see Figure 15.6).

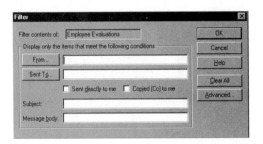

FIGURE 15.6 You can set conditions that items must match to be displayed in the folder.

9. Choose OK when you have finished setting up the criteria for displaying the contents of the folder.

Modify Views It's easy to make additional changes to any view you create by highlighting the view name and choosing Modify.

In this lesson you learned how to impose some rules and controls over a public folder you created. The next lesson discusses the Favorites folder, which is a way for you to simplify your access to public folders.

WORKING WITH THE FAVORITES FOLDER

In this lesson, you'll learn how to use a special folder, called a Favorites folder.

UNDERSTANDING THE FAVORITES FOLDER

As the various divisions, departments, and individuals in your organization create public folders for different uses, the list of public folders grows quite long. After a while it takes time and effort to scroll through all the public folders to find the one you need. And, many of the public folders are of little interest to you, either because you don't have a reason to use their contents, or you don't have permissions to access the contents. You still have to scroll through them, however.

Instead of crawling through all those public folders, you can use a special folder and use it for folder shortcuts to the public folders you need to access regularly. This special folder is called the Favorites folder.

Shortcut A shortcut is a reference to, or a pointer to, another object in Microsoft Exchange Server. That means that if you place a shortcut to a folder into your Favorites folder, the shortcut links to its connected folder. The folder itself is not placed in the Favorites folder (that would be a subfolder). Opening the shortcut causes the folder to open.

The Favorites folder is one of the folders placed under the Public Folders container during the installation of Microsoft Exchange Client (the other is a container named All Public Folders, below which all the public folders for your company are displayed).

ADDING FOLDERS TO THE FAVORITES FOLDER

After you know which public folders you need to access on a regular basis, you can add them to your Favorites folder. Just select the public folder and choose File, Add to Favorites (see Figure 16.1).

FIGURE 16.1   A click of the mouse is all it takes to add a public folder to your Favorites folder.

If you find that as new public folders are created, you're adding public folders to your Favorites folder often, save yourself some work by placing an **Add to Favorites** button on your toolbar. To do this, follow these steps:

1. Choose Tools, Customize Toolbar, to display the Customize Toolbar dialog box (see Figure 16.2).

FIGURE 16.2   Add buttons to the toolbar for quick access to menu items you use frequently.

2. Scroll through the list in the **Available buttons** box to find Add to Favorites, and click on it to highlight it.

3. Click Add to move this button to the **Toolbar buttons** box (you could also double-click on the button and skip this step).

4. Click on the Add to Favorites button in the **Toolbar buttons** box, then choose Move Up or Move Down to position it where you want it on the toolbar (the dialog box says up and down, but the toolbar is left to right, so think of up as left).

5. Click Close when you are finished. The **Add to Favorites** button appears on your toolbar.

ADDING SUBFOLDERS TO YOUR FAVORITES FOLDER

It's important to note that each public folder and subfolder is treated individually when it comes to adding it to your Favorites folder. If you add a folder that contains subfolders, only the folder itself is added. If you want to add the subfolder, you must go through the steps to add it. This means that when you look at the folders in your Favorites folder, you won't see a folder/subfolder scheme. In fact you won't be able to tell the difference between a folder and a subfolder, nor can you tell which subfolders belong to which folders (unless the person who created the public folder had the good sense to name any subfolders in a way that connects them to their parent folders).

USING THE FAVORITES FOLDER

When you want to check the public folders of importance, open your Favorites folder, which displays the list of all the public folders you're currently using (see Figure 16.3).

FIGURE 16.3   The Favorites folder lists your selected public folders.

Notice that one of the folders (Project X) in Figure 16.3 is listed with bold type. This means that the link between the shortcut in the Favorites folder and the original public folder has sent a message indicating there are new items in the public folder.

To see the items in the public folder, highlight the listing in the folders pane. The contents display in the contents pane, and unread items are listed in bold type.

When you look at the listing in the contents pane, you are looking at the items in the original public folder, just as if you had scrolled through the public folders to find the real one. The folder listing in the Favorites folder is merely a pointer, it is not really a folder so it has no contents.

REMOVING FOLDERS FROM THE FAVORITES FOLDER

There are going to be occasions when you no longer have to access a public folder—perhaps your participation in a project is finished, or you find that you really have no interest in a public folder you'd previously placed in the Favorites folder. You can delete the public folder from your Favorites folder by selecting it and pressing Del.

When you delete a public folder from your Favorites folder, you are only deleting the pointer, or link. The real public folder is not deleted.

You cannot delete the Favorites folder itself, it is a system folder.

In this lesson you learned about the Favorites folder. In the next lesson you'll learn about scheduling your time with Microsoft Exchange Client.

17

SCHEDULING YOUR TIME

In this lesson, you'll learn how to use the Schedule+ features in Microsoft Exchange Client to schedule your time and keep track of appointments.

Microsoft Schedule+ is a powerful software application capable of performing many tasks. It must be specifically installed on your computer as part of the installation of Microsoft Exchange Client. This lesson assumes that the Schedule+ software is installed, and discusses how you can keep your schedule of appointments in Schedule+.

GETTING TO SCHEDULE+

When you are viewing the Microsoft Exchange Client window and want to move to Schedule+, you learn you can't get there from here. There is no option for Schedule+ on any of the menu lists. You need to gain access to the Schedule+ toolbar button by following these steps:

1. Choose Customize, Toolbar from the Tools menu, to display the Customize Toolbar dialog box (see Figure 17.1).

2. Scroll through the list in the **Available buttons** box to find Show Schedule, and click on it to highlight it.

3. Choose Add to move this button to the **Toolbar buttons** box (you could also double-click on the button and skip this step).

4. Click on the Show Schedule button in the **Toolbar buttons** box, then choose Move Up or Move Down to position it where you want it on the toolbar (the dialog box

says up and down, but the toolbar is left to right, so think of up as left).

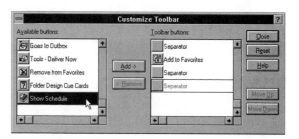

FIGURE 17.1   Use the Customize Toolbar dialog box to put the Schedule+ button on the toolbar—it's called Show Schedule.

5. Choose Close when you are finished. The Show Schedule button is now on the toolbar. Click on it to open Schedule+.

STARTING SCHEDULE+ FOR THE FIRST TIME

To use the features in Schedule+, you have to have a schedule file. The first time you use Schedule+ you'll be asked if you want to create a schedule file because one doesn't exist (see Figure 17.2). Follow the directions to complete the process.

Hereafter, just click the Show Schedule button to start the software.

THE SCHEDULE+ WINDOW

When you open Schedule+, the program window seems a bit busy and complicated (see Figure 17.3). However, it's really just a logical arrangement of views, which are different ways to look at the same information.

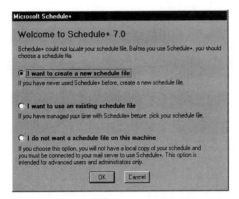

FIGURE 17.2   You have to create a schedule file to use Schedule+.

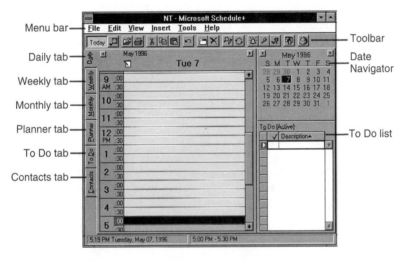

FIGURE 17.3   The Daily view of the Schedule+ window—move to another view by clicking the appropriate tab.

There are two elements on the window shown in Figure 17.3 that are unique to the Daily tab, and are not universal to all the available views: the Date Navigator and the To Do list.

ENTERING AN APPOINTMENT

To keep track of your time, and plan your work, you have to enter your appointments in Schedule+. This is accomplished by following these steps:

1. Make sure you're on the Daily tab (if you're looking at a different view, click on the Daily tab).

2. In the Date Navigator, move to the appropriate month (if the appointment is not in the current month), then click the day for the appointment. The Daily tab changes to that date.

 TIP **Moving Through the Date Navigator Calendar** The Date Navigator has two arrows, one in each of the upper corners. Click the right arrow to move ahead, one month at a time. Click the left arrow to move back one month at a time.

3. Click on the timeslot, or multiple timeslots, for your appointment to highlight that line.

4. Enter text that describes the appointment.

5. Click anywhere outside the appointment listing to end the entry process.

6. After the appointment is entered (see Figure 17.4), you will see a notation about it on all of the time tabs: Daily, Weekly and Monthly (the bell icon on the appointment line indicates the presence of the reminder).

By default, when you enter an appointment a reminder is attached to it (the bell icon on the appointment line indicates the presence of the reminder). That means you will see a note reminding you of the appointment ahead of time (that reminder interval is set by you).

FIGURE 17.4 The appointment is on the daily calendar—the bell means there will be a reminder.

If you don't want a reminder, you can click on the appointment line and then click on the Reminder button on the toolbar. This button toggles the feature, click on, click off.

You can also enter an appointment by clicking the New Appointment button on the toolbar (see Table 17.1 for more information about the toolbar buttons). If you use this method, an Appointment dialog box displays (see Figure 17.5).

In fact, when you enter an appointment directly onto the Daily schedule, as described earlier, there is actually an Appointment dialog box created in the background. You can see it (and make changes) by double-clicking on the left edge of the appointment listing.

VIEWING YOUR SCHEDULE FROM THE OTHER TABS

Click on the Weekly tab to see the appointments you've entered displayed in a Monday through Friday pattern (see Figure 17.6).

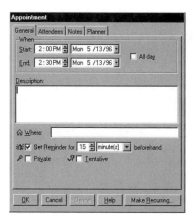

FIGURE 17.5   The Appointment dialog box lets you set options for appointments.

You can select an appointment and manipulate it with the toolbar buttons, or edit it by double-clicking and using the Appointment dialog box. Changes you make are reflected in every place this appointment appears.

FIGURE 17.6   The appointment you entered on the Daily tab appears on the Weekly tab.

If you click on the **Monthly** tab, any appointments you've entered appear in the appropriate date (see Figure 17.7). The notation is brief, but double-clicking on the entry displays the Appointment dialog box so you can see the details. You can also make changes to the appointment and those changes will be reflected everywhere the appointment is listed.

FIGURE 17.7   The Monthly tab displays appointments in a calendar form.

The Planner tab also displays an indication of your appointment (see Figure 17.8). This tab is only used to track your busy times and free times, so details about the appointment aren't displayed. The Planner also has a Date Navigator and an Attendees box so you can set up a meeting for a time that's convenient to all the attendees. Lesson 18 has information about setting up meetings with other users.

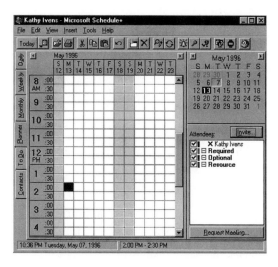

FIGURE 17.8   In the Planner tab, the block of time your appointment fills is marked to indicate you're busy at that time.

ADDING OPTIONS TO YOUR APPOINTMENT LISTING

There are a number of special features and options you can apply to an appointment after it has been entered. Some of them are available through the toolbar. Table 17.1 lists the toolbar buttons and their functions.

TABLE 17.1   TOOLBAR BUTTONS FOR SCHEDULE+

BUTTON	NAME	FUNCTION
Today	Today	Moves the schedule to today's date
	Go To Date	Opens a small Date Navigator Calendar
	Open	Opens another schedule file
	Print	Prints the schedule's data

continues

TABLE 17.1 CONTINUED

BUTTON	NAME	FUNCTION
	Cut	Moves selected text to the Clipboard
	Copy	Copies selected text to the Clipboard
	Paste	Pastes Clipboard contents
	Undo	Undoes the last action
	New	Opens a dialog box for a new entry—the entry changes to match the tab you're on (appointment, task, contact)
	Delete	Deletes the selected item
	Edit	Displays the Appointment dialog box so you can make changes
	Recurring	Makes the appointment a recurring one (daily, weekly, monthly, and so on).
	Reminder	Sets the reminder feature for this appointment
	Private	Hides the appointment from other users
	Tentative	Places the item in your schedule, but not in the schedule viewed by other users
	Meeting Wizard	Launches the Meeting Wizard, which walks you through the process of scheduling meetings with other users
	Timex Watch Wizard	Transmits data to a special Timex Watch you can purchase
	View Mail	Switches to the Microsoft Exchange Client window

There are other options for appointments available in the Options dialog box. Choose Option from the Tools menu to see the choices (see Figure 17.9). These are global options, meaning they are the default for every appointment you enter. Take some time to look them over, and also look at the options available on the Defaults tab. You may want to change your default settings if the current options don't suit you.

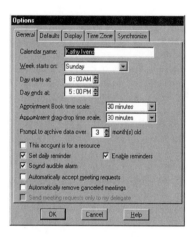

FIGURE 17.9   Set options about reminders, warnings, and other scheduling features with the Options dialog box.

SYNCHRONIZING YOUR SCHEDULE

A copy of your appointment schedule is kept on the server so that other users of Microsoft Exchange Server can learn when you're free or busy in order to schedule meetings. Exchange Server regularly checks your schedule to keep the network up to date on your plans.

In this lesson you learned how to open the Schedule+ software, enter an appointment, add options to appointment listings, and make a copy of your schedule available to other users. In the next lesson you'll learn how to set up meetings with other users.

18 LESSON

SETTING UP MEETINGS

In this lesson, you'll learn how to use Schedule+ to schedule meetings with other people in your organization.

Scheduling a meeting involves quite a few steps:

- You have to decide who should be there
- You have to find out when those people are available
- You have to select a meeting time convenient to all attendees
- You have to decide on a place for the meeting
- You have to notify all the attendees of the meeting's time and place
- You have to track the responses so you know how many (and which) attendees will be at your meeting

Whew! That's a lot of work. You won't have time to get much else done. Luckily, there are two features available in Microsoft Exchange Client that can make all of this faster and easier: the Microsoft Exchange Server Free/Busy folder, and the Microsoft Exchange Client Meeting Wizard.

Free/Busy   Microsoft Exchange Server has a container stored on the server called the Schedule+ Free/Busy folder. All users attached to that server have their Schedule+ meetings synchronized to this folder. The folder is replicated to other servers in the organization (and those servers also replicate their Free/Busy folders) so that it's possible to learn the free and busy times in every user's schedule.

Using the Meeting Wizard

The Meeting Wizard is a Microsoft Exchange Client feature that walks you through all the steps it takes to set up a meeting with other users. To use the Meeting Wizard, follow these steps:

1. Click the Meeting Wizard button on the toolbar. The Meeting Wizard opens as shown in Figure 18.1.

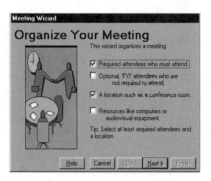

Figure 18.1   Specify the type of attendees and resources you'll need for this meeting.

2. On the first page (see Figure 18.1), select the options you need for this meeting. Then choose Next.

3. On the next page, click Pick Attendees to see a list of all users and select the required attendees. Choose Next.

4. If you specified a need for optional attendees, enter those names on this page, then choose Next.

5. Enter the location you want to use for your meeting. Choose Pick Locations to select a location from the Global Address List (double-click on the location to select it, then choose OK). Choose Next.

6. (Optional) You can enter more than one location and let the Wizard determine which to use (depending on availability). Choose Next.

7. (Optional) If you chose the option to schedule resources (such as computers or A/V equipment) in the opening Wizard page (refer to Figure 18.1), you will also have to select those resources here. The resource page follows the location page.

 TIP **Locations and Resources** It's important that companies create users and mailboxes for shared locations and resources. These facilities are used for meeting arrangements, and it's important to keep schedules for them. Locations are also used for sending e-mail. For example, the research library or the audio-visual room might want to send mail to users about new equipment, or users might want to send mail to the location requesting information about facilities. If there are conference rooms, equipment, or other similar facilities in your organization and they're not listed in the Global Address List, ask your administrator to remedy that.

Entering Nonexistent Names   If you enter a location or a resource that isn't listed in an address list, you can use the Check Names button.

This button is used to check typed entries against existing entries. If your entry isn't listed you are given the opportunity to add it to the address list. If you don't use the Check Names button and add the location or the resource to the address list, you'll have to do it later.

The Wizard won't complete the process and issue the invitations with any information that can't be confirmed against the users and locations known to your Microsoft Exchange Server system.

8. Enter the expected duration of the meeting and the travel time to the meeting. Choose Next.

Travel Time   The travel time is important. If you are holding the meeting outside of the office, give the attendees an indication of how long it will take to arrive at the meeting place so that when attendees' schedules are checked the travel time can be factored into the decision about their availability.

9. Enter the acceptable times and days for this meeting (see Figure 18.2). This information is matched against the free and busy times of the attendees. Choose Next.

10. (Optional) If there were optional attendees specified for this meeting (refer to Figure 18.1), the Wizard asks if their free/busy schedule should be checked. If you're listing them because you merely want them to know that the meeting is taking place, answer No. If you want them to attend (if they're free), answer Yes. This affects the Wizard's determination of a good meeting time.

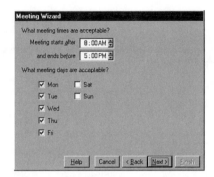

FIGURE 18.2   Specify a range for the start and end times, and select the acceptable days, for your meeting.

Now that you've entered all the information, the Wizard takes over. The entities involved in your meeting plan (attendees, locations, and resources) are checked for free and busy times. If any entity has not been diligent about keeping a schedule, the Wizard will report that fact. Figure 18.3 shows a report on a problem location, and Figure 18.4 reports a problem with an attendee. Just click OK on any of these informational dialog boxes.

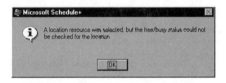

FIGURE 18.3   The people in charge of the conference room haven't made a schedule so the server's free/busy folder has no information.

USING THE WIZARD'S RESULTS

When all the free/busy schedules have been checked, the Meeting Wizard displays the information it has gathered (see Figure 18.5).

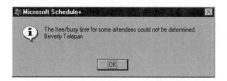

FIGURE 18.4   Users who don't keep schedules make it difficult to schedule meetings.

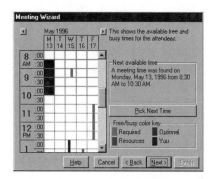

FIGURE 18.5   Free and busy times are displayed and a meeting time is suggested by the Meeting Wizard.

Most of the time, unless all the attendees you selected are incredibly busy people, the Meeting Wizard offers you a choice of meeting times. The original Wizard report displays the next available time that all the criteria you set for attendees and resources are met.

You can look at another possible meeting time by choosing Pick Next Time. Additional meeting dates are displayed, in chronological order. If you want to go back to the original meeting date, click the left arrow at the top of the calendar that displays the free/busy times.

> **Do It Yourself**   In case you don't like any of the times the Wizard picked, you can view the free/busy information for all the attendees and resources. There's a color code key on the dialog box, so you can decide which attendee or which resource you want to give up to have the meeting on a date that doesn't match all the schedules. To schedule this meeting, however, you'll have to issue the invitation messages manually.

When you have selected one of the Wizard's proposed dates, choose Next. The Meet Wizard's last page displays to announce that the Wizard has done its job, and to tell you that the next step is to issue the invitations to all the attendees. Choose Finish.

Sending the Invitations

The Meeting Request form automatically displays when the Meeting Wizard finishes (see Figure 18.6). All the information necessary to notify the attendees is already filled in (optional attendees are in the Cc box). If you want to, you can add a note to the text. Click on the Send button to send the meeting notice. The meeting is also added to your schedule.

In this lesson you learned how to use the Meeting Wizard to set up a meeting based on the attendees' free and busy times. In the next lesson, you'll learn how to use Schedule+ to manage your tasks and projects.

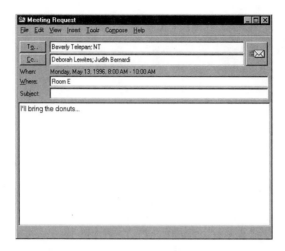

FIGURE 18.6   All the necessary information is already filled in when the Meeting Request form appears.

19 MANAGING TASKS

In this lesson, you'll learn how to use the Schedule+ software to track tasks and projects. You'll learn how to enter tasks into your To Do list and how to connect tasks with specific projects.

A *task* is an item in a list of things to do. It can be related to a project or it can be an independent chore that you're responsible for. Tasks also can be recurring; for example, you may have to turn in an expense report every month, or send out invoices every week.

ADDING TASKS TO YOUR TO DO LIST

To track a task, you need to tell your Microsoft Exchange Client system about it. There are actually two ways to add a task: quick and easy, which inserts the task into your To Do list; less quick, but more detailed, which lets you set a priority, end date, and other information about the task.

QUICK TASK ENTRY

The fast way to insert a task into your To Do list is to use the Daily tab (which is in the foreground by default when you first launch Schedule+). Then follow these steps:

1. Click the To Do section of the Daily tab.

2. Click the first available row (the row is highlighted as soon as you click on it).

3. Type in a name or description of the task (see Figure 19.1).

4. Press Enter.

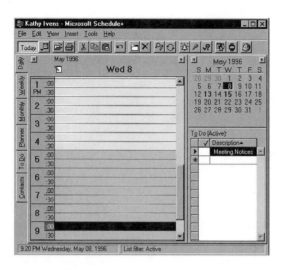

FIGURE 19.1   You can enter a task in the To Do list of the Daily tab.

When you enter a task in this quick way, there are certain defaults assumed about the task's characteristics. The task is assigned to the current date (the date displayed in the Daily tab), has a priority of 3 (see the discussion on priority later in this lesson), and has a duration of one day.

QUICK TASK COMPLETION NOTIFICATION

There's also a quick way to tell Schedule+ that you've finished a task. Click the box to the left of the task description on the Daily tab, indicating you've completed this chore (see Figure 19.2). That column to the left of the description is the "check off" column that displays a check mark when a task is done.

ADDING TASKS WITH DETAILS ATTACHED

If the task is a bit more complicated, and needs to be configured for a date range, or a priority, or other details, you can provide this information by using the Task dialog box to set up the task. Just follow these steps to create your task:

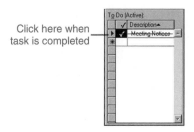

Click here when task is completed

FIGURE 19.2   Check off the task when it's completed.

1. Click the To Do tab (see Figure 19.3).

FIGURE 19.3   The To Do tab displays the tasks you're tracking, along with information about them.

2. Click the Insert New Task button to display the Task dialog box (see Figure 19.4).

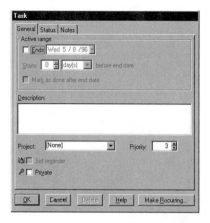

FIGURE 19.4   The Task dialog box lets you configure a task with many options.

3. If the task will take more than a day, select Ends, then specify the date on which the task will end (you can click on the down arrow next to the entry box to see a Date Navigator, from which you can select a date).

4. In the **Starts** box, specify the number of days, weeks, or months before the end date that the task starts. (Click the down arrow to choose between days, weeks, or months.) This is the task start date.

5. Select Mark as done after end date, if this task definitely ends on the specified end date.

6. Use the **Description** entry box to type a brief description of the task.

7. In the **Project** box, enter the name of the project to which this task is linked (if there is one). You can enter a new project if you want to, or choose an existing project from the list that displays when you click the arrow to the right of the entry box.

8. Use the **Priority** box to set the level of importance for this task. Use the up and down arrows to scroll through the priority choices.

TIP   **Task Priority Levels**   As you scroll through the priority choices available, you'll see the numbers 1 through 9, and the letters A through Z. The numbers display on the right side of the Priority box, the letters display to the left. You can take advantage of this by creating all sorts of priority schemes, even including choosing a letter, then choosing a number, to end up with a priority such as C3. It's a good idea to work with other people in your company to establish some predetermined meanings for all the available priority indications.

9. Select Set reminder to enable the reminder feature. When you select this option, two additional selection boxes display to let you specify the number of minutes, hours, days, weeks, or months before the start date (or the end date) you want to see a reminder.

10. Select Private if you don't want this task to be seen by other users on the network.

11. (Optional) You can choose Make Recurring if this task fits that category.

12. When you are finished, click OK. The task now is listed on your To Do list.

Managing Projects

A *project* is a goal-oriented group of tasks. For example, you can have tasks such as "collect budgets from department heads," "import General Ledger into database," and other related tasks as part of the project called "Budget Review for 3rd Quarter." After you've created your project, you can link your tasks to it by using the

Task dialog box (refer to Figure 19.4), as described in the previous section.

There are two methods for adding a Project to your To Do list:

- Enter a project name into the **Project** box of a Task dialog box (as described in the previous section), which gives the project a default priority of 3.

- Choose Insert, Project and use the Project dialog box to give the project a name and a priority (see Figure 19.5).

FIGURE 19.5   Use the Project dialog box to give the project a title and a priority.

Project names appear in bold on the To Do list and their priority levels are indicated in parentheses. You can click the plus (+) button next to the project name to see the list of tasks linked to the project.

There are some things to know about the relationship between projects and their linked tasks:

- The priority for a project is not automatically inherited by its tasks—each of the tasks can have whatever priority you choose.

- If you make the project private, all of the tasks linked to the project are also made private.

In this lesson you learned how to add tasks to your To Do list, and you also learned about projects and the way to link tasks to projects. In the next lesson you'll learn how to use Schedule+ to manage the information about the people you do business with (contacts).

20 MANAGING CONTACTS

In this lesson, you'll learn how to use the Schedule+ software to track and manage all the people you contact for business or for personal reasons. You'll also learn how to use the information you accumulate in a productive way.

The jargon for this type of software is "contact management" and it's more than just a little black book. You can use your contact listings for fast entry of appointments or tasks related to specific contacts, or you can group contacts who share a common bond, and therefore, you know who has to be contacted when a particular issue arises.

ENTERING CONTACTS

To enter information about a contact, move to the Contacts tab and click the Insert New Contact button on the toolbar. This brings up the Contact dialog box (see Figure 20.1), which is divided into four sections.

You can move between the sections by clicking the section tabs:

Use the **Business** tab to enter information about this contact. The fields are self-explanatory (refer to Figure 20.1).

Use the **Phone** tab to track all the phone numbers for this contact (see Figure 20.2).

When you look at either the Business tab or the Phone tab, you see icons that look like a telephone. If you have a telephone attached to your modem, you can click one of the telephone icons and your modem will dial the number next to the icon. Your modem line is now a voice line, and you will be prompted to lift the receiver to talk with the person you called.

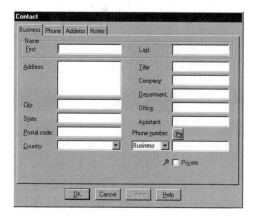

FIGURE 20.1   The Business tab of the Contact dialog box lets you enter information about this contact.

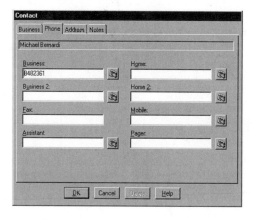

FIGURE 20.2   You can track every type of telephone number for a contact.

(Of course, you have to have a telephone instrument attached to your modem to take advantage of this feature.)

The contact's name is placed in a *calling log* as part of your contact tracking efforts (see Figure 20.3).

FIGURE 20.3   If you have a modem you can call this contact with a click of the mouse.

Calling Log   When you click on a telephone icon to make a call to a contact, a log is kept. The log's file name is CALLLOG.TXT and it can be found in the directory where your Windows operating system is installed. This is a plain text file and you can open it with any text editor (or any of the text word processors that came with your operating system). There is a line of text for each call you made to a contact, including the name, telephone number, date, time, and duration of the call. You should make sure to edit this file occasionally so it doesn't grow too large to work with comfortably.

The **Address** tab provides a place to store a home address and phone number for this contact, in addition to the spouse's name, the contact's birthday and the date of the couple's anniversary.

The **Notes** tab is a place for you to write comments or notes to yourself about this contact. In addition, this tab provides four user-definable fields (named **User 1** through **User 4**), which you can use to enter data that helps you sort your contact list.

For example, you might decide to use the User 1 field to indicate your relationship with this contact. You can invent codes so that the data you enter in User 1 is consistent, such as Family, Customer, Vendor, and so on. Then you can select contacts by code to produce a list you can use for a specific purpose.

After you've completed filling out the information in the Contact dialog box, click OK. The name is added to the list on the Contacts tab (see Figure 20.4).

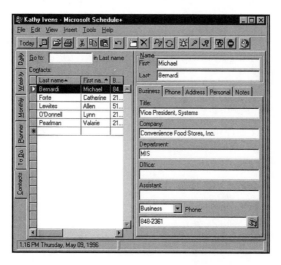

FIGURE 20.4   Click on a name to see details displayed on the right side of the window.

The list is on the left side of the window. When you select a contact in the list, details about that contact are displayed on the right side of the window. You can click on any of the tabs to display the information you need.

 TIP   **Quick Contact Entry**   You can also enter information about a new contact right at the Contacts tab listing. Just click on the first blank row, enter the last name, press Tab, and then enter the first name. You can then enter the detailed information in the appropriate places on the right side of the window.

CONNECTING TASKS WITH CONTACTS

If you need to follow up with a contact, perhaps by making another telephone call, or sending some information, you can create a task that's connected to the contact. To do this, follow these steps:

1. Click on the appropriate contact name to select it.

2. Click the right mouse button to see the shortcut menu.

3. Choose Task from Contact.

4. When the Task dialog box opens, the contact's name is in the Description box (see Figure 20.5).

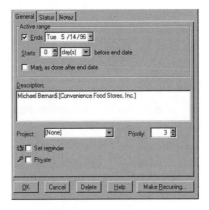

FIGURE 20.5 You can link a task to a contact from the right-button context menu, and the contact name is automatically inserted in the Description box.

5. Enter additional text to remind you of the task (for example, add the word "call" in front of the contact's name).

6. Set the date for the task and any priority specifications you need, then click OK.

CONNECTING APPOINTMENTS WITH CONTACTS

In much the same way as connecting a task with a contact, you can use the right-button context menu to connect an appointment with a contact. To try it, follow these steps:

1. Click on the contact name to select it. Click the right mouse button to see the context menu.

2. Choose Appt. from Contact on the context menu. The Appointment dialog box opens with the contact's name in the Description box.

3. Specify the date, time, and place.

4. (Optional) Set a reminder if you want to.

5. Click on the Attendees tab to add any additional attendees.

6. Click OK when you have finished entering information into the dialog box. The appointment is displayed in your schedule.

7. (Optional) If you have invited additional attendees, a Meeting Request message form displays with the attendees in the To box and all the necessary information already filled in. You can add a note if you want to, then click on the Send button.

SORTING YOUR CONTACTS LIST

You can sort the contacts in your Contacts list by several criteria. To establish a sorting scheme follow these steps:

1. Choose View, Sort to display the Sort dialog box (see Figure 20.6).

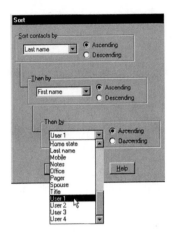

FIGURE 20.6   You can choose any category to sort and sub-sort your contacts list.

2. Select a category for each of the three levels of sorting (**Sort Contacts by, Then by, Then by**). All the categories from all the tabs of the Contact dialog box are available as sort options.

3. Specify whether you want **Ascending** or **Descending** sorting for each level.

4. Click OK when you are finished. Your contact listing is sorted by the categories you selected.

TIP   **Only One Sort Level Is Required**   You don't have to use all three sorting levels when you design your sorting scheme. There is a choice of "none" available and you can select it for level 3 (or both level 2 and level 3) if you want to.

The sorting scheme you design becomes the default for your Contacts tab.

TIP   **Quick Sort**   When you enter new names on blank lines of your Contacts list and after you've completed all your entries, choose View, Sort Now. The new entries are placed on the list according to your default sorting scheme.

In this lesson you learned how to enter and manage contacts, and how to link those contacts to tasks and appointments. In the next lesson you'll learn about delegating mail functions so that others can take over some of your e-mail chores (or the other way around).

DELEGATING MAIL FUNCTIONS

In this lesson, you'll learn how to delegate mailbox functions so that you can arrange to have someone else take care of some or all of your e-mail. And you'll learn how you can take care of another user's mail.

Delegating mail is useful if you're out of the office and need your mail attended to, but it also can be helpful to delegate some mail duties to an assistant. It's the same function that assistants have provided for years with the mail that's delivered through the United States Postal Service. The mail is sorted, opened, and frequently answered with a standard response.

UNDERSTANDING DELEGATION

Delegation is the process of permitting someone to represent you. In Microsoft Exchange Client, you can arrange to have a delegate do one or all of the following things:

- Open your mailbox and view the contents. You can make arrangements to be notified about those messages which are important and then decide whether the delegate should respond to them.

- Send mail on your behalf, which means that messages sent from your mailbox by the delegate have the delegate's name along with the words "on behalf of" followed by your name in the From field of the message.

- Send mail in your name, which means that messages sent from your mailbox by the delegate have your name as the sender. The receiver has no reason to think the mail is not from you.

To delegate responsibilities, you have to perform two separate operations: You must give the delegate access to your mailbox; then you must specifically configure your mailbox to permit the delegate to send mail in your behalf. If you also want the delegate to send mail in your name, you must have an administrator make configuration changes to your mailbox at the server; you cannot provide that right yourself.

PROVIDING ACCESS TO YOUR MAILBOX

To have a delegate access your mailbox (or specific folders in your mailbox) you must configure your mailbox for the necessary permissions. To accomplish this, follow these steps:

1. In the folder pane of your Microsoft Exchange Client window, select your mailbox (if you only are giving permission for a specific folder, such as the Inbox, select the folder).

2. Right-click the mailbox, then choose Properties from the context menu to bring up the Mailbox Properties dialog box.

3. Click on the Permissions tab (see Figure 21.1).

4. Choose Add to see the Global Address List, then double-click on the delegate's name. You can name more than one delegate if you want to. Click OK when you are finished adding names.

5. The delegate's name appears on the Permissions tab.

6. Select (highlight) the delegate's name and then choose a role. Click the down arrow to the right of the Roles entry box to see the choices, and select the appropriate one. Choose OK to close the dialog box.

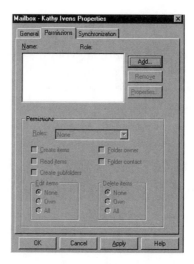

FIGURE 21.1   Use the Permissions tab to give specific rights to your mailbox to other users.

HANDLING CONFIDENTIAL MAIL

If you're used to having an assistant or secretary open all your mail, and want to extend this duty to e-mail, there's no way to exclude confidential or personal items. (For snail mail, there's usually a "personal" or "confidential" note on the envelope to prevent anyone else from opening it.) You can fix this by having the administrator create a second mailbox for you to use for receiving personal mail, making it a hidden mailbox.

 Hidden Mailbox   Microsoft Exchange Server provides a way for an administrator to hide a mailbox, which means it isn't displayed on any address lists. However, if senders type in the mailbox name when they're filling out the To section of a message, the message will get to the mailbox. To use this feature, you have to give the hidden mailbox name to anyone who needs to send you confidential mail, and then check that mailbox yourself.

ACCESSING ANOTHER USER'S MAILBOX

If you have permission to access another user's mailbox, you have to take these few steps:

1. Choose Tools, Services to display the list of services installed in your profile.

2. Select Microsoft Exchange Server and choose Properties.

3. Click on the Advanced tab to move to that page (see Figure 21.2).

FIGURE 21.2 You can add the capability to open additional mailboxes if you've been given the permissions.

4. Choose Add to add another item to **Open these additional mailboxes**.

5. Enter the name of the additional mailbox you've been given permission to access.

6. Click OK. Then click OK twice more to close the dialog box.

7. Your folder list now displays the additional mailbox along with your own mailbox (see Figure 21.3).

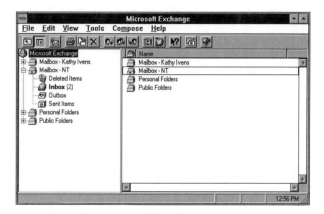

Figure 21.3 The folder pane shows all the mailboxes to which you have access.

You can manipulate the new mailbox the same way you handle your own mailbox.

Delegating the Send Mail Function

When you let a delegate send mail on your behalf, the **From** field of all messages sent by this delegate will contain the words **Sent On Behalf Of** followed by your name, along with the delegate's name.

To authorize a user to send mail on your behalf follow these steps:

1. Choose Tools, Options.

2. Click the Exchange Server tab of the Options dialog box (see Figure 21.4).

3. Choose Add to place a delegate's name in the box titled **Give Send on Behalf Of permission to**. Select a name from the address list that's displayed, and double-click on it.

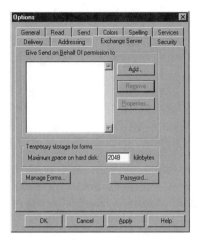

FIGURE 21.4 Choose a delegate to send mail throughout the system on your behalf.

4. Repeat this to add additional delegates. Click OK when you are finished. Then click OK again to close the dialog box.

SENDING MAIL AS A DELEGATE

After all the permissions are set, your delegate can begin sending mail on your behalf (or in your name if the administrator has configured this option for you). Of course, if you are the delegate, then this section shows you how to send mail on another user's behalf.

Sending mail on another user's behalf is accomplished from your own mailbox. It's just like sending a message from yourself to another user, except you have to change the name in the From field. To send mail on another user's behalf, follow these steps:

1. Click on the New Message button to open a new message form. By default, this form does not display a **From** box in the header, so you have to remedy that.

2. Choose View, From Box to insert a **From** box in the message window.

3. Move your pointer to the **From** box and either type in the other user's name or click on From and select the name when the Global Address list displays. You do not have to add anything else, Microsoft Exchange Server takes care of adding the information that this message is written on behalf of the other user.

4. Fill in the rest of the message header, placing the recipient's name in the **To** box, additional recipients in the **Cc** box, and filling in the **Subject** box.

5. Move to the text box and enter the message.

6. Click on the Send button to send the message.

That's all there is to it. Figure 21.5 shows what the message looks like when it is opened by the recipient.

Figure 21.5 The recipient can tell that you sent the message on behalf of someone else.

If you didn't have the proper permissions to fill in the From box with another user's name, Microsoft Exchange Server will issue an error message and refuse to send the message.

Of course, if the administrator had established delegation rights for sending mail in the name of the user, the recipient would not be able to tell that the delegate composed and sent the message. The From box would merely give the user's name.

In this lesson you learned how to give permissions for others to access your mailbox, and how to send mail on behalf of others. In the next lesson you'll learn how to use the Inbox Assistant to automate some of the tasks you perform when you receive mail.

USING THE INBOX ASSISTANT

In this lesson, you'll learn how to manage incoming mail with automatic procedures, using the Microsoft Exchange Server feature called Inbox Assistant.

The Inbox Assistant provides a way for you to establish automatic procedures that are performed on all your incoming mail. Some of the actions you can accomplish automatically are:

- Reply to incoming mail under certain conditions that you establish

- File incoming mail in specific folders using criteria you establish

- Forward incoming mail under certain conditions that you establish

You can use the Inbox Assistant to manage your mail whether or not you have your Microsoft Exchange Client software open; the work is accomplished at the server (where your mailbox is located).

There are two things you have to do to put the Inbox Assistant to work:

- Create a set of conditions (called rules) for the Inbox Assistant to look for when it examines incoming mail

- Create a set of actions for the Inbox Assistant to begin whenever the conditions have been met

CREATING RULES

Creating a rule is a simple process, and there are an enormous number of permutations and combinations you can invent to cover all the possibilities. This lesson creates a scenario that tells the Inbox Assistant that whenever a message comes from the Payroll department, you want it moved to a specific folder in your mailbox. That's because you've given permission to an associate for that folder, and that associate takes care of all the timesheets and other payroll issues for you. You can accomplish this by following these steps:

1. Choose Tools, Inbox Assistant to display the Inbox Assistant dialog box.

2. Choose Add Rule, which brings up the Edit Rule dialog box (see Figure 22.1).

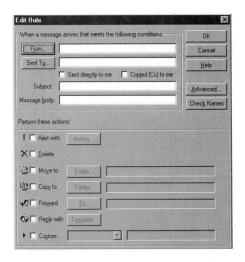

FIGURE 22.1 The Edit Rule dialog box lets you configure the rules and the resulting actions for the Inbox Assistant.

3. In the top part of the dialog box (**When a message arrives that meets the following conditions**) specify the conditions that the message has to meet to qualify for

any action to occur. In this case, that means that the message is from the Payroll department.

Narrowing the Rule   You'll have to do some homework for some of these rules to work. For example, in this scenario you might have a user named Payroll, which is a mailbox shared by all members of the Payroll department; you might have one member of the Payroll department who is the only person that ever sends e-mail about payroll issues; or you might have to list every person in the Payroll department just to make sure you've covered all the possibilities.

4. Click on From to indicate you want to base this rule on the sender. Then select the appropriate name(s) from the Global Address List by double-clicking on the name in the list. You can select as many names as you want to, and click OK when you are finished.

5. Choose an action from the bottom section of the dialog box (**Perform these actions**). In this case, choose Move to, then click on Folder. The Move Message To dialog box appears, as shown in Figure 22.2.

6. From the Move Message To dialog box, choose the folder you want to move these messages into.

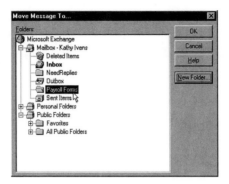

FIGURE 22.2   You can automatically move a message into any folder in your Microsoft Exchange Server system.

TIP

Picking a Folder   You can choose any folder in your Microsoft Exchange Server system as the target for moving or copying messages. If you pick a mailbox folder or a public folder, Microsoft Exchange Server will take care of the move for you regardless of whether you're working in Microsoft Exchange Client at your computer. If you choose a personal folder (which resides on your local hard drive) Microsoft Exchange Server will not complete the Inbox Assistant's work until you launch your software and are connected to the server. At that point, the message is moved into the chosen personal folder.

7. Click OK, then click OK again to close the Edit Rule dialog box. The new rule is listed in the Inbox Assistant dialog box (see Figure 22.3).

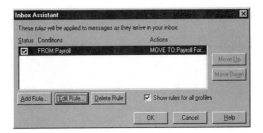

FIGURE 22.3   All the rules you create are listed in the Inbox Assistant dialog box.

Set Multiple Rules   This exercise was a simple one: set one rule, have one condition. You can, however, set multiple rules. Perhaps you want a rule that says "if the message is from Payroll and the subject is Overtime Reports, perform this action." Just continue to set rules until all your conditions are established.

TURNING OFF A RULE

If you want to abandon a rule temporarily for some reason (perhaps your assistant is on vacation and you'll have to take care of all your mail yourself), you don't have to delete the rule and then re-create it. The Status box for each rule can be selected or deselected to toggle the rule off and on (refer to Figure 22.3).

In this lesson you learned how to set conditions and actions for automatic mail handling by the Inbox Assistant. In the next lesson you'll learn how to use the Out of Office assistant to automate mail handling when you're not at work.

USING THE OUT OF OFFICE ASSISTANT

23

In this lesson, you'll learn how to use the Out of Office Assistant to manage your incoming mail automatically when you're not in your office.

If you're going to be out of your office you can use the Out of Office Assistant to deal with incoming mail. For example, you could automatically send a note to each person who sends you mail, saying you're away and giving instructions ("contact Bob in my absence"). Or, you could forward a copy of all (or certain) messages to a coworker.

Like the Inbox Assistant discussed in Lesson 22, you have to create rules for the Out of Office Assistant to follow.

SENDING OUT OF OFFICE NOTES

The most common use of the Out of Office Assistant is to instruct it to send a note back to every person who sends you e-mail. The note, which you compose, can inform the sender of your absence, ask the sender to contact someone else, or say whatever else you might want to say. The Out of Office Assistant keeps track of the names of senders and only sends one note to each person.

To have the Out of Office Assistant send a notification to everyone who sends you e-mail during your absence, follow these steps:

1. Choose Tools, Out of Office Assistant to bring up the Out of Office Assistant dialog box.

2. Put your cursor in the **AutoReply** text box and enter the message you want to send to people who send you mail in your absence (see Figure 23.1).

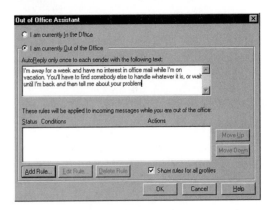

FIGURE 23.1   Enter a message for the Out of Office Assistant to send while you're away from your office.

CREATING AUTOMATIC RULES

You also can create a set of rules for automatic handling of your incoming mail while you're away from your office. The rules can be applied in addition to the AutoReply feature.

FORWARDING MAIL

One of the common practices is to make sure that messages that have a high priority attached to them are forwarded to another user for instant action. To establish this rule, follow these steps:

1. From the Out of Office Assistant dialog box, choose Add Rule.

2. When the Edit Rule dialog box appears, choose Advanced.

3. From the Advanced dialog box (see Figure 23.2), select Importance, then choose High from the list box of priority choices. Click OK.

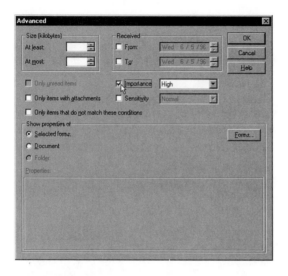

FIGURE 23.2   You can set specifications for the kind of messages you want handled automatically while you're away.

4. Choose an action from the **Perform these actions** section of the Edit Rule dialog box. In this case, choose Forward, then click the To button and select (double-click) the user who will receive this message. Then choose OK.

5. The rule appears in the Out of Office Assistant dialog box (see Figure 23.3).

6. Neither the rule nor the AutoReply feature will be implemented until you select the **I am currently Out of the Office** option button in the Out of Office Assistant dialog box. Click OK to close the Out of Office Assistant dialog box.

CREATING OTHER RULES

Arranging for high-priority messages to be forwarded is a simple process. While you go through it, however, notice the other choices for conditions and actions "The principles for establishing more complicated rules and actions are the same and it shouldn't be difficult for you to establish more complicated criteria to take care of your needs.

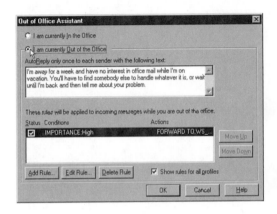

Figure 23.3   The AutoReply and any rules you've set will only go into effect when you're out of the office.

Returning to Work

After you return to your office, when you launch your Microsoft Exchange Client software, you'll be reminded that the Out of Office Assistant is enabled (the **I am currently Out of the Office** button is selected). Open the Out of Office Assistant and select the **I am currently In the Office** option button.

Conflicting Rules   If you've enabled the Inbox Assistant, it's always in effect. If any of the rules you establish in the Out of Office Assistant conflict with the rules in the Inbox Assistant, during the time you are out of the office the Out of Office Assistant rules will take precedence.

In this lesson you learned how to use the Out of Office Assistant to handle incoming mail when you are not in your office. In the next lesson you'll learn how to set up your Microsoft Exchange Client software so you can work at a different computer, either at home or on the road.

WORKING OFFLINE

In this lesson, you'll learn how to take all the steps necessary to work from an offsite location.

Working *offline* is when you're not connected to your network server because you're offsite. When you're not at the office you have to have some tools available that let you work on a remote computer and then later (when you're back in the office) get the information on your office computer matched up with your off-site computer.

UNDERSTANDING OFFLINE COMPUTING

When you're working in Microsoft Exchange Client at your office, you're connected to a Microsoft Exchange server computer and the two computers interact continuously. When you work at home, or when you're traveling, you can't connect to the server with cable. You are offline.

When you are offline, there are elements of your Exchange system to which you don't have access. Your Microsoft Exchange Client window (the viewer) displays a number of objects in the folder pane, and it combines those objects that are on the server with those that reside on your local hard drive. When you're offline, the objects that are stored on the server aren't available. The server objects are your mailbox (and all its folders), and all the public folders. The only components that are on your local drive are the personal folders you created.

To take care of this situation, Microsoft Exchange has developed a set of tools that let you work on some of these folders on a remote computer, then either dial in from an offsite location to connect to the server, or connect to the server when you return to the office and synchronize the contents of your folders.

PREPARING TO WORK OFFLINE

You have to set up your Microsoft Exchange Client software to prepare for working offline. This is not difficult and should only take a few minutes.

There are two steps involved in getting ready to work offline:

- You need to prepare the computer you'll be using offline by installing the Microsoft Exchange Client software

- While you're connected to the network, you need to tell Microsoft Exchange Client that certain folders must be available for offline work

If you're using a portable computer, you usually can connect to the network (or your office computer for access to the network) through cables. From a home computer, or other offsite computer, you'll have to connect via telephone lines. Have the administrator assist you in setting up the hardware and software necessary to use these connections.

PREPARING THE OFFLINE COMPUTER

Install Microsoft Exchange Client on the computer you'll use offline, which is usually a portable computer you use when traveling, but may be a desktop computer at your home.

PREPARING FOR OFFLINE FOLDERS

An offline folder is a replica of a folder that is stored on the server. Mailbox folders and Favorite folders are the folders available for offline work.

You have to tell Microsoft Exchange Client that a folder (or multiple folders) will be used offline. This is done so that the system knows it has to synchronize the offline folder with the folder on your office computer. You only have to do this once.

 Synchronize   Normally, when you copy a file or folder back and forth between computers, the contents of the source file replace the contents of the target file. Synchronization, however, is a process by which Exchange looks at the contents of both folders, then places information in both so the contents are identical. This means you can work offline, and also work online, and then you can synchronize your work so that both folders have all the work you've done in both places.

To make a folder available offline, follow these steps:

1. Right-click on the mailbox or Favorite folder that you want to make available offline.

2. Choose Properties from the context menu, then click on the Synchronization tab of the Properties dialog box (see Figure 24.1).

3. In the **This folder is available** section, select When offline or online. Then choose OK.

4. When the information dialog box about the offline folder file appears (see Figure 24.2), click Yes to create the file.

5. When the Offline Folder File Settings dialog box appears (see Figure 24.3), you need to choose a file name and an encryption scheme.

6. Choose an encryption scheme for the file, or choose to have no encryption.

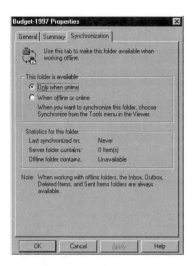

FIGURE 24.1   The online/offline choices and information about synchronization are found in the folder's Properties dialog box.

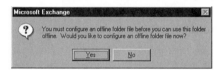

FIGURE 24.2   The offline folder file is necessary to synchronize offline folder contents to online folder contents.

FIGURE 24.3   You have to establish the configuration for your offline folder file.

Encryption Exchange can encrypt the file so it cannot be read outside of the Microsoft Exchange Client software. The choice between the two encryption schemes should be made depending on if you are using file compression on your hard drive. If you do, choose compressable encryption.

7. Accept the default name EXCHANGE.OST for the offline folder file. If the system administrator feels a different file name should be chosen, enter that.

8. Click OK when you have made your choices, and Microsoft Exchange Client creates the file.

DOWNLOADING THE ADDRESS BOOK

To work offline, you should have an address book on your offline computer. The address book, of course, is kept on the server. When you are working offline and can't get to the server, you'll need a copy of the address book so when you click on a button to see a list of users, the information is available. You can download the address book by following these steps:

1. On the Tools menu, place the pointer on Synchronize to display the submenu, then choose Download Address Book.

2. Choose the format for the address book from the Download Offline Address Book dialog box (see Figure 24.4). Your options are:

- Choose Download offline address book to move all the data in the address book to your hard drive. Select this choice if you want details about users (such as telephone numbers, titles, and so on), or if you are going to be sending encrypted messages.

- Choose Download offline address book without details information if you only need access to mailbox names.

3. Click OK.

FIGURE 24.4   You can choose whether to download all the details in the address book.

Now, when you work offline, the address book is available. This means you can run Microsoft Exchange Client, compose messages, place files into folders, and do many of the tasks you do when you're in the office, connected to the network. The difference is, everything is being stored on your offline computer instead of being placed on the server.

COMING BACK ONLINE

When you reconnect to the server, and you launch Microsoft Exchange Client, the syncronization process will make sure the folders contain identical items, and you can send the mail you composed to all the appropriate user mailboxes.

In this lesson you learned how to establish the tools to work offline on a computer that isn't permanently connected to your network.

INDEX

Check out Que® Books on the World Wide Web
http://www.mcp.com/que

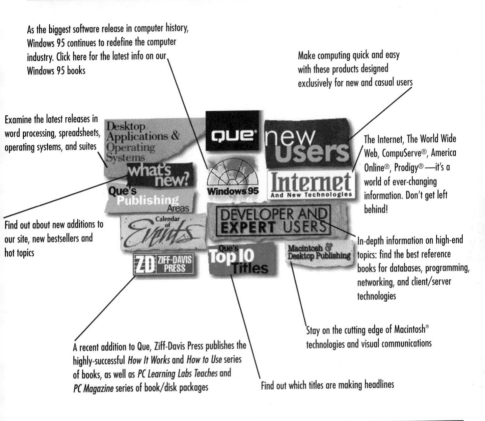

As the biggest software release in computer history, Windows 95 continues to redefine the computer industry. Click here for the latest info on our Windows 95 books

Make computing quick and easy with these products designed exclusively for new and casual users

Examine the latest releases in word processing, spreadsheets, operating systems, and suites

The Internet, The World Wide Web, CompuServe®, America Online®, Prodigy® —it's a world of ever-changing information. Don't get left behind!

Find out about new additions to our site, new bestsellers and hot topics

In-depth information on high-end topics: find the best reference books for databases, programming, networking, and client/server technologies

A recent addition to Que, Ziff-Davis Press publishes the highly-successful *How It Works* and *How to Use* series of books, as well as *PC Learning Labs Teaches* and *PC Magazine* series of book/disk packages

Stay on the cutting edge of Macintosh® technologies and visual communications

Find out which titles are making headlines

With 6 separate publishing groups, Que develops products for many specific market segments and areas of computer technology. Explore our Web Site and you'll find information on best-selling titles, newly published titles, upcoming products, authors, and much more.

- Stay informed on the latest industry trends and products available
- Visit our online bookstore for the latest information and editions
- Download software from Que's library of the best shareware and freeware

QUE® has the right choice for every computer user

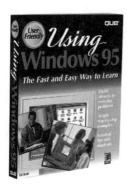

From the new computer user to the advanced programmer, we've got the right computer book for you. Our user-friendly *Using* series offers just the information you need to perform specific tasks quickly and move onto other things. And, for computer users ready to advance to new levels, QUE *Special Edition Using* books, the perfect all-in-one resource— and recognized authority on detailed reference information.

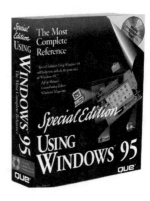

The *Using* series for casual users

Who should use this book?

Everyday users who:

- Work with computers in the office or at home
- Are familiar with computers but not in love with technology
- Just want to "get the job done"
- Don't want to read a lot of material

The user-friendly reference

- The fastest access to the one best way to get things done
- Bite-sized information for quick and easy reference
- Nontechnical approach in plain English
- Real-world analogies to explain new concepts
- Troubleshooting tips to help solve problems
- Visual elements and screen pictures that reinforce topics
- Expert authors who are experienced in training and instruction

Special Edition Using for accomplished users

Who should use this book?

Proficient computer users who:

- Have a more technical understanding of computers
- Are interested in technological trends
- Want in-depth reference information
- Prefer more detailed explanations and examples

The most complete reference

- Thorough explanations of various ways to perform tasks
- In-depth coverage of all topics
- Technical information cross-referenced for easy access
- Professional tips, tricks, and shortcuts for experienced users
- Advanced troubleshooting information with alternative approaches
- Visual elements and screen pictures that reinforce topics
- Technically qualified authors who are experts in their fields
- "Techniques form the Pros" sections with advice from well-known computer professionals

Complete and Return this Card
for a *FREE* Computer Book Catalog

Thank you for purchasing this book! You have purchased a
superior computer book written expressly for your needs. To
continue to provide the kind of up-to-date, pertinent coverage
you've come to expect from us, we need to hear from you.
Please take a minute to complete and return this self-addressed,
postage-paid form. In return, we'll send you a free catalog of all
our computer books on topics ranging from word processing to
programming and the internet.

Mr. ☐   Mrs. ☐   Ms. ☐   Dr. ☐

Name (first) ☐☐☐☐☐☐☐☐☐ (M.I.) ☐ (last) ☐☐☐☐☐☐☐☐☐☐☐☐☐☐

Address ☐☐☐☐☐☐☐☐☐☐☐☐☐☐☐☐☐☐☐☐☐☐☐☐☐☐
        ☐☐☐☐☐☐☐☐☐☐☐☐☐☐☐☐☐☐☐☐☐☐☐☐☐☐

City ☐☐☐☐☐☐☐☐☐☐☐☐ State ☐☐ Zip ☐☐☐☐☐ ☐☐☐☐

Phone ☐☐☐ ☐☐☐ ☐☐☐☐ Fax ☐☐☐ ☐☐☐ ☐☐☐☐

Company Name ☐☐☐☐☐☐☐☐☐☐☐☐☐☐☐☐☐☐☐☐☐☐☐☐☐☐

E-mail address ☐☐☐☐☐☐☐☐☐☐☐☐☐☐☐☐☐☐☐☐☐☐☐☐☐

1. Please check at least (3) influencing factors for purchasing this book.

Front or back cover information on book ☐
Special approach to the content ☐
Completeness of content ☐
Author's reputation ☐
Publisher's reputation ☐
Book cover design or layout ☐
Index or table of contents of book ☐
Price of book ☐
Special effects, graphics, illustrations ☐
Other (Please specify): _____ ☐

2. How did you first learn about this book?

Internet Site ☐
Saw in Macmillan Computer
  Publishing catalog ☐
Recommended by store personnel ☐
Saw the book on bookshelf at store ☐
Recommended by a friend ☐
Received advertisement in the mail ☐
Saw an advertisement in: _____ ☐
Read book review in: _____ ☐
Other (Please specify): _____ ☐

3. How many computer books have you purchased in the last six months?

This book only ☐   3 to 5 books ☐
2 books ☐   More than 5 ☐

4. Where did you purchase this book?

Bookstore ☐
Computer Store ☐
Consumer Electronics Store ☐
Department Store ☐
Office Club ☐
Warehouse Club ☐
Mail Order ☐
Direct from Publisher ☐
Internet site ☐
Other (Please specify): _____ ☐

5. How long have you been using a computer?

Less than 6 months ☐   6 months to a year ☐
1 to 3 years ☐   More than 3 years ☐

6. What is your level of experience with personal computers and with the subject of this book?

	With PC's	With subject of book
New	☐	☐
Casual	☐	☐
Accomplished	☐	☐
Expert	☐	☐

Source Code — ISBN: 0-7897-0897-3

7. Which of the following best describes your job title?

Administrative Assistant .... ☐
Coordinator .... ☐
Manager/Supervisor .... ☐
Director .... ☐
Vice President .... ☐
President/CEO/COO .... ☐
Lawyer/Doctor/Medical Professional .... ☐
Teacher/Educator/Trainer .... ☐
Engineer/Technician .... ☐
Consultant .... ☐
Not employed/Student/Retired .... ☐
Other (Please specify): .... ☐

8. Which of the following best describes the area of the company your job title falls under?

Accounting .... ☐
Engineering .... ☐
Manufacturing .... ☐
Marketing .... ☐
Operations .... ☐
Sales.. ☐
Other (Please specify): .... ☐

9. What is your age?

Under 20 .... ☐
21-29 .... ☐
30-39 .... ☐
40-49 .... ☐
50-59 .... ☐
60-over .... ☐

10. Are you:

Male .... ☐
Female .... ☐

11. Which computer publications do you read regularly? (Please list)

_____
_____
_____
_____
_____
_____
_____
_____
_____
_____

Comments: _____

_____
_____

Fold here and scotch-tape to mail

᚛᚛᚛᚛᚛᚛᚛᚛᚛᚛᚛᚛᚛᚛᚛᚛᚛᚛᚛᚛᚛